I Have A Poem For You

Poems by
Charles Shively

Edited by
James Dunn and Erik Lomen

Bootstrap Press
2025

ISBN 13: 978-1-946741-18-9

First edition. First Printing.

Cover photo by Walta Borawski.

Bootsrap Press
Lowell, MA & Mills River, NC

www.bootstrappress.org

Editors Note

The first three sections of this book were typeset from three previously unpublished manuscripts of Charley Shively's poetry. The text ahead remains as close to the original justification as we could get. Obvious mispellings and indentations were retained after seeing them repeated in handwritten form, early typed form and retyped form, all stapled together and organized within Charley's papers in the Beinecke library at Yale. We feel that the mispellings, indentation complexity and scattered oddities lend themselves to Charley's pure anarchist heart, spirit and poetic mind. The tricky dichotomy of publishing this collection is that Charley might have loved it but likely would have hated it simultaniously. Perhaps the unfinished is the ultimate state of such a radical human that was Charles Shively.

CONTENTS

INTRODUCTION

I got to know Charley and his work through my involvement with Jack Powers and Stone Soup in the 1990s where Charley and I were featured poets there together several times. Stone Soup and its offshoot the Beacon Hill Free School had been important venues for both Charley and John Wieners. In 1973, Wieners was the guest editor of the Stone soup magazine. Among the many poets in the issue—Wieners himself, Joe Dunn, Steve Jonas, Lee Harwood and Jack, he included Charley Shively. When Charley first wrote to Wieners while Wieners was institutionalized in 1969, he sent him a poem, writing to him as one admiring poet to another. It was the beginning of life-long friendship in poetry between the two that would last until John's death in 2002. John was always supportive of Charley's poetry. A few months before John's passing, *Van Gogh's Ear* published both John's and Charley's work amongst many other notable poets. The magazine also published a handwritten letter from Wieners urging the publishers to include three poets whom John admired greatly—Robin Blaser, Tom Meyer and Charley Shively.

In April 1997, we took a magical road trip. A few weeks after Allen Ginsberg died, John Wieners was scheduled to read with Robert Creeley at the Andy Warhol Museum to celebrate the opening of a Francesca Clemente exhibit curated by Raymond Foye. The three of us took off from Boston in Shively's station wagon. The trip was reminiscent of the road trip Charley and John took in a VW Bug in 1972 to deliver a list of demands for Gay Liberation at the Democratic Convention in Miami.

We first stopped in Philadelphia for a reading and appreciation of John Wieners's work at the Kelly's Writer House at the University of Pennsylvania. Before the reading, John, Charley and I spent the day roaming around Philadelphia and Camden. Charley's two books on Walt Whitman were breakthroughs in the realm of Whitman criticism and I had referred to them often in my studies of Whitman. The three of us drove over the Ben Franklin bridge to Mickle Street in Camden and found the row house in a decimated part of a forgotten city across the street from the NJ transit bus terminal. We were the only ones there when the National Parks Guide answered our knock at the door. Wieners chose to wait in the car. When I told the guide that Charley was a respected Whitman scholar, he became very excited and gave us the royal treatment paying special attention to Charley during the tour of the house. On our way out of town we paid our respects at Whitman's grave, Charley telling stories of his lovers and telling stories of Whitman and his many lovers as we stood at the cemetery gate of Whitman's mausoleum.

We stopped in at the legendary bookstore Giovanni's Room where the staff welcomed them both like celebrities. We paid a visit to the Action Aids agency (now called Action Wellness) in downtown Philly where my mother was the executive director. We spent several hours with the staff and met personally with patients who received their services. Both John and Charley dazzled the whole crew with their grace and humor.

Charley was a poet at heart and wrote and published poetry throughout his life. As far back as his undergraduate days at Harvard, he wrote copious amount of poetry, as Michael Bronski points out in The Last Gay Liberationist—"Poetry was, for him, a form of sanity-a religious person might say salvation—that broke out of the mundane rigors of poverty, work, and the labors of the academy." His poetry was quite different from the influential anarchist essays he wrote—however, his mission as a poet and poetry publisher reinforced his belief that queer poetry should also be an act of revolution—not an assimilation into the existing hierarchy of the poetry establishment. He believed that poetry and art offer a way of being both political and culturally emancipated, of fighting the revolution, and of realizing self-expression "Every faggot poet fights then on two fronts. You can't just be a queer poet; you must destroy the existing profession of poetry. You can't just be a good queer 'citizen,' you must destroy the state."

He created a community of poets devoted to a poetics of queer otherness, whose work by virtue of its very existence was an act of liberation, solidarity and revolution. His dedication to poetry and other queer poets outside the mainstream remained steadfast throughout his life. His belief in total freedom of the poet was essential to his publishing work and to his approach to his own poetry as he states in the article *JohnJob, Editing Behind the State Capitol or Cincinnati Pike*, "As one of the Good Gay Poets Collective, I saw our publishing as a way of bringing total freedom to our authors, allowing each of us to write whatever and however we wished. What we needed most was not respect from the straight world but respect for each other's work." He explained his appreciation of poets and his approach to poetry in the Afterword he wrote for John Wieners journal, *A New Book from Rome*: "Poets may be arranged/deranged differently or why would they ever write the way they do? Poetry itself is a form of ecstasy, madness, and disorder, which may well frighten the poet him/herself and their audiences. There is certainly an unhappy widespread wish to be 'normal.' And while most might secretly admire the 'abnormal,' still they fear being seen as different or 'odd'."

He was a founding member of the Fag Rag Collective and the Good Gay Poets Collective (the name a takeoff on Walt Whitman's nickname The Good Gray Poet) publishing several seminal books of poetry by queer poets outside the mainstream poetry establishment such as Freddie Greenfield's *Were You Always a Criminal?* ruth weiss's *Desert Journals*, Aaron Shurin's broadside *Exorcism of the straight/man/demon* and John Wiener's magnum opus, *Behind the State Capitol*. Shively also published Adrian Stanford's groundbreaking *Black and Queer*, the first book of American poetry written by an out, gay, African American poet. Even though the press published a wide array of renegade queer poets, Good Gay Poets only published one book of Shively's poetry, even though he had many manuscripts of his own work. That book *Nuestra Senora de los Dolores: the San Francisco Experience*, a slim volume titled in Spanish, was published in 1975 as a joint book with Salvatore Farinella's *The Orange Telephone*.

Shively's work is sparse, surreal and mystical, a rush of images in lean language and form. John Wieners' poetry was a major influence on Charley's work. However, their poetry in content and form are markedly different. Charley once told me that that the key to understanding John's work was realizing John was a Surrealist. Charley's poetry also has elements of Surrealism but in a much different form than Wieners' work. His poems at first seem like hallucinogenic and surreal streams of consciousness, sometimes referred to as "Emily Dickinson poems on LSD." But there are deeper and more urgent flashes of brilliance fused throughout his work when read closely that charge them with a vibrancy and rhythm, especially when read aloud. Charley was a performative poet. He read the poems with a conviction and with a theatrical delivery that still resonates when I read the poems on the page. His voice part W.C. Fields, part Mae West, unique and quirky, brought his poems to life as he sang out with conviction.

Charley was among the poets and musicians who read Allen Ginsberg's *Howl* at the Aerosmith bar in Boston for a local radio station recording and broadcast. The bar was packed with a rock n roll crowd and the whole reading was recorded to be played on the radio later. Charley arrived late and was tasked with reading, *Footnote to Howl*. He approached the microphone without any hesitation delivering the most stunning and brilliant incantation of HOLY HOLY—his voice insistent with a rhythmic cadence enchanting the mesmerized crowd. He delivered it with conviction, and the bewitching charm of a Southern preacher or a fevered auctioneer—he was an anarchist at heart and his performance was incendiary.

Charley's house on Broadway Terrace just outside of Harvard Square was a rambling purple funhouse of sorts. The beauty of Charley was that you could stop by anytime and he would greet you warmly in a terry cloth robe and would always be up for a visit with whomever I brought along with me. Charley would regal us at all hours of night or day with his tales of sexual adventure and any discussion on politics, poetry, and anarchy. The list of poets and friends that came along to visit Charley is long and varied –it was important to make those connections. Charley grew more eccentric from the time I met in in the early nineties, but his conviction, his sense of humor, and his dedication to poetry and poets, never wavered.

James Dunn
Beverly, MA
June 6, 2025

STONELICKS
BEYOND OHIO

PRIMAL STEM

1.

just seems like
yesterday
you were born
chicken coup wire
knife desire quiet
purple pill hatching
dye scrambled
halftone fried
hair cropped
peach stained
musical window cut
porch insect screen
hung out hand face wrinkled
tired waiting in line
lace voice
hiss escapes
antique glass
ushered sermon
limousine smiles
gray half heel shoe
doctor mending waiting
flashlight kerosene brass
traction midnight vesper
red bank cyclone
shoe factory last
chance upper sole
mother grandmother
cedar box sliced off
thumb trigger finger
stitched blood hinged
placenta tongue salted
recalling rulers feeling new
birth force
farce face
flesh pain
pushed out
pig butchered
headcheese in
a yellow crock
over cellar stair
drain chilled
clogged barge

scalding water
blackberry brandy
lip synchronization

2.

ragweed seed
perennial cosmos
root line rhizome
thru two thigh high

hedge row balls
iris edged blade
thick skin peeling
off skinny dip ledges

arena music
organ massage
no map potatoes
in between roadway

pistiled pee pie
phallus penis pod
of okra pulpit parka
chambered cock anus pit

ocher excrement
liquid epidermal
shy achievements
in goldenrod petals

strong stem guide
in double railing
wall seams struck
proprioceptive

perineum dawn
interurinal et
feces nascimur
always liked it

that way in quick pumpkin
skinned brimestone pickles

GRANDMA'S SIDEBOARD

grandmother's sideboard
copper teakettle wicker
hair handled gargoyle
kerosene lamp burnt
fresh cut glass
ivory mantelpiece
stashed drawer opening

apricot seed
peaches lying
in uncounted rows

gashed sharp eye
scar only cats
see no more now

painted throat fallen
white marble stained
greatseal soft coat
pressed tin ceiling
purple spider skin
black shoe broach
antique mirror

glued table kindling chip
half split hickory stems
she'd want it that way
without blinds behind
rayon lavender shroud
maple door unhinged
scarab scrap quilt

ten pound breast
sewn ancient luxury
doctor knew too late
mother's milk disease
afraid of stork stone bills
dying miles outside landscape

cut down stub
frozen burnt tub
pink blooms return
cherries in applesauce
giant angel winged begonia

SECRET GARDEN

some dangerous
places left to
        rest
        in peace
        Erie Street
        faces shattered

broken up cup
edge chipped
        gone up
        in flames
                crimes

according
to whose law
        and orders
        commandments on
        optional borderline

broken equipment
        fatigued
        alternative
        roads feigning
        closed arguments

fallen apart
goose feather
        pillows
        allowing
        no eyebrow

strawberries
not to escape nor
        leave detection of
        unwritten footprints
        from invisible inkwells

between unwished
words hiding
beyond all
        utterance
        contradiction

not yet becoming

one wit wiser for
never having gone
            nearer wavering
            Baltimore & Ohio
underpass
overpriced
            products
            destroyed in their
own lurid expectations
what to
remember is
never to look
back nor forward
but to get away quick

MEANWHILE

meanwhile blue
tile lake laid
back in a minute
            Canute
            absolute

gold river eyes
drink one glass
silver stream rush
            hush
            little baby

body bag weight
infancy entrance
lazy leg journey
            back fence
            legacy brings

rum running
mittens outside
inside patterned
            hatters gone
            after glowing

hogs all called home
to where lost shadows
borrow open wheelbarrow
            unbuttoned
            bottomed

tub stool stalk
tall tale walking
trails bent sideways
          talking it up
          and laughing

more square yard
two time by four
cotton waist bands
          inside land
          shadowed sand

RESTRAINT RETRIEVAL/ENEMIES OF EMILY

words left and right
split tongue peels run off with
walking vegetables learning
          to pee
          straight
          leaf seed
          soft maple
          overlaying
          red on yellow

too slippery
cannot tell
          (time
          o'clock
          years
          fears)
          a lie
          to die for
          life not easy
                    chatter
                    splatter
                    scattering
looks at it one way
falling foliage views
          autumn forest
          corpse close
          to formless
          trees being held
          together by threadbare
          Smyth sewn perfect binding

saddle stitched
passage quotations of
whole books in unmapped
stain shaded covers open
lavender kingdoms
to dine on
another
coastal
invasion
air search
circulation
land location
confessional walking
judgment
uncertainty
whose friends
all will steal
whole libraries
to conceal missing
manuscript pages of
pasted up soul memory
commotion is so emotional
split spilled and unrecovered
across towns spreading
too mean to stay put
stand pat
cheat plunder
tablecloth labels
grandmother's lovers
alphabetized
surely someone
knows retrieval
storage
security
misplaced mistraced
New Paltz
New Jersey
New Lebanon
New Harmony
eggs over hominy
all you can eat

had another new moon
around Saturn swallowed
how often full
everything spun

scattered pieces
from astronomy
shoulders slipped
unmarked undisguised
shelves collapsed tattooed
abandoned full volume guitar
entering deeper sleeves
suddenly open payments
more promised
relationships
appointments
affections
scheduled
endurance
unnoted
debts
fade away from all
relief outline reviewed
references pointing to
a malpractice suit
against doing hard
time every jeweled
splendor glittering
dissolves red
untraced mineral
watermark delighted

no matter how nunb unnumbered
pages remain retain old
addresses disconnected
some never can come
back anyway would
they really want
letting go desire
to give away
attachments
gadgets
gifts
in unused bits of wet cloth
transparent bubble salt
embroidered pillow scrap soap
trunk lid latched
picture perfect
decoupage
erasure daily
decomposition

perfumed collages
stuffed together
someday sundown dowry
completely unknown
never even repaid
in one big lump sum

ceremony wherever begun
resembling severance
beads forgotten blend
in tulip wings zippered

tight lip record
lost places
mind lists
somehow this
lifeline lasts
on unflipped pages only so long before
unremembered dismemberments disappear
(And who isn't this dedicated to?)

GREASY

atelier liberty burnt
hole undershirt hair
used part workshop

bolt duct rivet
rubber hose slips
red steel toolbox
told what metals mix
heating welding tools
watching out for blind
driver's warning lights

Crosby Field construction
Colrain Avenue school bus
corporations in pursuit

lost part bin
tap beer drawn
screwdriver lips
torn racing forms
ending even doweled
clip worn wann wallet half gallon solder rings

advanced mathematics works
odds against chance leaking
one hundred old refrigerators
broken door latches frozen tight

freon greasy
cap fingernail
wide saw tooth
emery stone oil
spark hole grime
tree branch trunk
cut socket wrenches

dropped bomb cast
niece reaches beyond
unemployed navy dungaree
horn both hung
lime spiked wall
thirty-seven car
bought brand new
engine block rust
caulking crevices
scraped getting by
hot iron stove pipe

Shooting Utility Pole
Insulators Is Illegal
And Very Dangerous

rough nail
run on while
slipping into
wooden wicker
smooth handled

orange paradise
at long last left hand
daddy rests in peace

MONARCH BULLET APPROACH

reappeared
butterfly
dye rubbed
orange clay
black charcoal

milk come
and go truck
driver farming
all night stops
at exactly midnight

bare ass
beer brown un-
armed and
a bandit one
two three or more

simple damp
floor sampled
timing is
everything
in place gone

plow bone
silver buckle
stone bed
spring loam
stairwell makeup
eyes see
water again
against scenery
punctuation
purification
clarification

given indirect evidence of
tunes fallen asleep while
driven blind behind time

GOING HOME ALONE

turn dis-
traction hip
broken three
o'clock
afternoon

phone call
can't talk
here no time

medicine
broken door

will un-
til quiet
street going
back over
country lanes

made up
city girl
plain speaking
spring
flowering

metal ring
solder wired
forever finger
comes
so soon

time hardly
left nothing
to say **hang**
in there
is no rest

risk after all
is said and
done every
word heard
just once

in a lifetime
stops collapsed
in released time

OAK OFTEN OPENED

out trap
trip drift
wishes swift
fish
dish
fresh

water salt
faultless quarter
hand stands startled
    under
    bundles
    unbordered

slate ledged
gate guarded
later grins
    find
    binary
    boundaried

stone phones
wireless grounded
baritone on fire
    saxophone
    home rule
    party line

dime dreams
creamed in frames
loosened timing gear
    tears
    fear
    beer

crushed hush
washed away
little baby
pleases freeze
framework fleeced

    buttons open
    outside bottom
    ready to get up
    and go out to play
        and stay far away

EVEN STEPHEN

leaves
shadows
please don't

go now
or later

beg borrow
steel knives
driven by
crazy noisy
silent

wordless thieves
afraid lovers
of too much
property
to handle

given away
alcohol under
glass grain
sandstone
houses

stand
or sit in
undone justice
hard time
to come

bicycle
spokesperson
prisoner
of lost
hands up

deposition
disposition
dispossession
all one
kettle of
of frying crying
baby fish burned
never stepped
twice into
same oven

cinder vice
child flames

charm
karakul
charcoal

what is never
done will be
for tomorrow
another
hot day

SENSELESS INNERTUBES

on Christy's farm
hidden baby breath
purple corn flower
scorching horn blown
dandelions annihilate
grinning chrysanthemum
horned daffodil battalions

drill thistle
rough floorboard
gladiola smoking
gardenias chasing
stabbed snapdragon
alfalfa clover covered
lovers lie backhanded in

copper coiled fields of
alphabetic running up
blue morning glories
between lined thread
nylon bolt stud boots
folded inside box feet
of jack-o-lantern cistern

dahlia unseed
birdbath swallowed
red funnel cucumber
fence-line barn rose
sassafras bark burnt hot
flaming ashes blush blooms
into pasture field moonlight

SCARCELY DESERVED PARTIALITY

"Mr. Wordsworth is
fond of the hollyhock"
—Margaret Fuller

stained glass
trees of them
dry straw beds
unfenced plain
    unspoken
    avenue
    lanes

gathered deep clay blond
    high rise white
    wet crinoline
    brown crimson
    pink muscle
    rust rose
    straw color

hidden plant
purse pearl
proselyte
coin seed
    waves heated
    hard over hand
    parchment held head

paths bend
between two
green division
gravel pits open
over six feet tall
accidents thrown up
against wire-link fence

    lines between silk sheets
    tickle licking liking
    uncovered neighbors
    on pillow feathers
        inside Billy Budd
        anus goat stretched
        hollyhock windows open

ANUS RADIUS

eat that
leash bone
honey leaded
heart's breath
        without blood
        in mud eyed
        even fields

burst playing
lost strawberry
blue burnt tipped
over lingering cusp
        purple leaf
        berry filled
        cream covered
ears bend
back frozen
shooting tongue
foot first month
        broken day
        nodding out on
        maple park paths

through open mauve
climbing vines
clinging free
in forevermore
        last night
        under water
        tasting right

drinking more than
enough willowed weed
free tree uncovered loss
never having been unwilling
        to take any
        cutting thorn
        sighing throngs

sing of
threadbare
wet weaned can
opening begging
annual anvil iron

bulbs breaking
arrive in spring

SUEY SUEY

pigsty door
open anal eye
hairbrush
frail trail
leans on bone
guardian man cramp

framed inside
flesh lashed
sutured
structure
slop bucket
alluring suet

crack pinsetters
enter sphincter
ear sigh
sow's purse
candle sings
following tallow

mud sucking
sweat swallowed
dry dust
underbrush
hollow August
branches waving on

bush hill echo
filled with leaf
shaken heart
shaped birth
unmarked canal
shadows straying

bottom back top stuck
loafing under foot
uphill and
fun bowling
on dirt floor
time gone down

lean-to peach
tile roof beaten
skin foreknowledge
sandstone yellow rock
saddle burnt into soundless
skin whispers for another round

REMBRANDT RED

butchered bull
run while you
        can calf cattle
        car carpenter cap
        le couloir a lentilles

bone cavity rose
sprung throat deep
        ripe rope sponge
        raw red resting on
        two pimiento threaded

saucer dish
ladle cupped
        cone core
        coup de cock
        corks unscrewed

spread eagle
without a wing
        wet worn
        weeping warm
        not yet ready

to go on inside
before saying hello
        marked up
        monk can never
        take another Monday

freeze dried
obsidian timed
        thigh twine
        throat thorn
        thought stops

please master
slain platter
        rib cage
        stone cap
        blue starred
        struggle ends

Venus rises
steam before
power lines on
golden medallion
curled hair anise eyes
rubbed already gone along
alighted downstream gardens

HORSEHAIR COUCH

bird cave-in
can you arm
robbery bed
motion rock
cradle wing
home alone
blue cycle

big horn
fly light
wind burnt
saddle sit
glide shady
still water
brow crowned

eye waist
come ready
or not feet
level bread
bacon backs up
without getting warm
at breakneck speed
        early climb
        phone called
        to please cherry

twin tree eyed
guards standing

covered in ivy chime
charmed tank level cartwheel
covered golden pine finish
        in unposted side
        pasture fields
        come over here
        right away now

on covered bridge
hideaways of
just enough
open sorrow

pen talk
long silent
prison walls
at last heard
can never open
until all opposite
cymbaled chambers play dead

HIS BODY IN MINE

duck eye
silent wait-
ing slaughter
        not one
        word said

motorcycle
to abattoir
imperfect doors
        of perception
        better never opened

wheel spinning
ace of spades
roulette card
        sparkling on
        heaven's door

at precisely
three one afternoon
        in wet Hanoi
        feathers resist
        this weeping weather

feet claw
yellow scales
bound for glory
        another story
        of waiting love

lost in
translation
going over Red
        River water
        without speaking

thin broken sword
swallowed swimming
bottomless throats not
        opened before
        time collapses
inside Bae Mai Hospital
mother near her last
        breath in never
        stop street
        traffic

of another place
karaoke playing
        Michael Jackson
        thrilling **beat it**
                ventriloquists

speak of being her
Lafayette Paris
Magenta parlor
        Hotel granting
        All good wishes

(for Alice Notley)

GRAND HOTEL

sharp eye
to tell all
truth tooth
says nothing

more grass

burns jumps
into flame's
own frying pan

paintbrush
breathless with
every left step
keeping time lost

starts right off
   center foot
   slide lines
   drawn in sand's

grand eye
known snort
around town
word spreading
drunk sleeps
deep in shadows
equal under shrinking
pink fluffed pillow slips

on alto drops
looking be-
yond sight
clock fallen

bartender
Grand Hotel
watches water
turn into wine

SUBSOIL SHADOWS

some dangerous
places left to
   rest in
   peace on
   Erie Street

cup broken
edges chipped
   gone up
   in flames
   a crime

according
to whose law
        and order
        commandment on
        an optional border

equipment devoured
        unfatigued
        alternative
        roads feign
                an argument

fallen apart
on goose feather
        pillows
        allowing
        eye-brewed

strawberry stencils
not to escape now nor
        ever live in detention
        by unwritten footprints
        on invisible inkwells

between wishes
words go astray
        beyond all
        utterance
        contradiction

can never become
one wit wiser for
never having gone
        nearer wavering
        Headgates Road
                over spliced
                underpass

products destroyed inside
high speed expectations
        of what to not
        remembered is to
        never look back
                nor forward but
                to get away quick

KNUCKLE UNCLE

wild hollow
porkchop hill
pumpkins swing
in windows struggle
        stumbling Uncle
        Roy James glider
        toe part cut off

corncob
corn row
corncrib
corn silk
corn shock
corn stalked
fields of corn

cornucopia
cornbread
corn shuck
corn picker
cornstarched
corn whiskey
shelling corn

cornfed
corn bin
corn dogs
corn thistle
shucking off husk
cornered corn holing

clay clod
tan **khaki** pant
windy hairy stubble
held together in back

field hands
eat it all packed
in tin can Old Vienna
skinless *au jus* sausages

HALF-ACRE ROAD

corn hole
lazy bowls
crazy crying
          trying to
          dry it

hit miss
hot spot
broken hope
          untaken
          shaken

against dreams
trains come
down here
in tears
fears

baby bean
grown too soon
beyond prime
          pine
          behind

drawn into
sweet straw
weather shelter
          can warm
          tan ankle

peg chains
begging pooch
porch floorboards
to slope towards
          approval

at pearly
gate doors
open going bang
          all alone
          out of town
          in Bethlehem

FLORAL PLAY

not sunflower

yellow knife
bright piece
except stalk
frond dusted
nutty seed
grand fan

nor rose

except soft
kiss folded
bud heads
extended
to you all
blushing

not fern

except arm
tent runner
fiddle heads
more pores
on tentacle
underground green
submerged testicles

not iris

haunched inside
crouched fear
broach scarab
sacred cover
rhizome root
expect tears
looking up

nor bridle breath

floating unexpected
chorus wandering into
scattering shattered clouds
snow free

in late May on
one way sheer sheets

not dahlia

sudden flower gloss
except dark gloved
cloud wet burst
plant spout
grandmother's
bright colored
washboard band playing

not zinnia

brilliant straw
simple singer
country music
bleach smell
tan respite
well colored
for best revenge

nor Sweet William

although loved
uncle knew no
undershirt pale
moon died too soon
in purple hung light
dark globes now too late
in shattered spectaculars

not piney peony

overexposed
exploded pod
hot extravagance
with just a little
bit of jumping over fences
on released parting borders

nor sharp gladiola

cedar tree lightning
in need of more time

expecting serried poplar
coffin funeral showy stick
stark stalk naked stagecraft

nor morning glory

wood back porch
bluebird wanders
heartless gutter
can't look twice
broken eaves open
into one way mirrored
names imagining another

crawling behind barns
staying open all night
little heavy bead seeds
early morning four-o-clock
planted over and over again
without second thoughts of eye
extended throat by heart hands eaten

columbine climbs
treacherously embroidered

asterisk
pansy pastel
Queen Ann lace
tulips disguised
in wild west roses
roaring blue aphasia
between syllabled fields

leave rhubarb
breathless weave
almost crystalline
pale purple dazzling
memories of snapdragons
syntaxed on asparagus tips
off of red lacquered radish

wheeled violet trellis
early summer lettuce
growing wild winged
scallion rutabaga
where everything

iris rhymes or
is deciduous
aster vocabulary
simple delphinium
no one understands
ever blooming willow
willing fuchsia taken
into dangling negatives
by incomplete participles

BATAVIA LUST

boundary bafflement
prison yard birds on
deer feet
in water
beyond inland
pleasure tides
in grain seekers
of only on shore lines
open unmeasured keepers of
today's released escape valve

fireplace
wild alarm
enflames armed
struggle after all
these years
watchers at
birthday party
foundation creamed
grease paint dream disguises
burnt down suddenly old barn doors
switch sex into open swimming pools

lilac sea
weeds carry
sweetener nearer
William's open landing
by mouth or upriver
taking it all or left
only to be washed away
wheel thrill paddled axe
come back in camel nostrils
el dorado incommunicado asks and
receives crumbs just trying to help

dawn yawns
come in ink
drinking well
unbitten unbridled
ready or not morning
after hours gathering in
gravel bed train lines alive and
well turning back from downtown Batavia

LANDSCAPE IN SEARCH OF WARREN HARDING

continuous drawers
uncoil rubber
drum rolls
unfolding

  half spoons full
  legs lift hiss piss
  latched on table leg
  unmatched with cup or
  milk saucer cupboard door
  lost chemical air pressure
  colors bonded blend randomly

each piece sticks to
glued splintered bulbs
on floral painted walls

  shout sprout root
  settled jelly jar
  cellar light apple
  rolling insider bubbles
  spread budding grove bench
  stretched on willing screens
  waiting to catch fallen crumbs

whatever goes in
mixed with notes
stays somewhere

  time catching its lipless
  rest bar break area where
  two strain melodies flow
  in piano accompaniment

sounding boards up
ending uncaptured
emotion elusive
sift
swift
shifts
sniffs
snap
snarled
sound cracks in
beveled bowl
level
shovel
trebled
several

high clef
deft motionless
pillow
andante
adelanto
weatherproof
pull
pin
pinch
pick up
water ways
contain
stretched
incontinent
always contending

for more
hard to come
by back bruises

CHICKEN HOUSE

April hatch
baby chicken
pretzel footed
blue pill feeder
rouge raw dry cob
floor raised up eye
leveled drinking water

drying shuck
corncrib slat
milk open weed
slanted sideways
red clover lovers
leftover stub fields
point seed pods to explode

bailing wire
curled teased
straw shepherd
pine unpainted
barn door wheel
stalked dandelions
on tongues hanging in

sandy south craw
fried drum drawn
blind hen killed
    broken picnic
    stick twisted
    neck bleeding
    breast liver

dog taste
fowl blood
shot because
always unforgotten

one drop can last
forever they say having
once licked their chops in

hen house tin
sheet stapled
paper shingled
green petal tar
slat single side
slide dumped Wilson Milk
cans and Karo empty bottle

cow stall hay
loft stacked
empty shelf

one leg at a
strip teasing
time when every
thing seems newer

pumpkin silage
time to fly on
tin roof fodder
green bean fence
hedge shed ready
clover only three
inches lost in air

Junior's goat
eaten tincan
squirted milk
face lick white
covered at a great
distance burning old roses
in long border rows grow quicker

CRISTY'S WATERMELON DAYS

bushtree boy
whipping lilac
pants down tongued
        drip dry
        thighs leave

lost limb logs
hung out to dry
ice should never be
        beaten
        so swift

ditch deep
sitting eating
ripe crop stock
        escaping
        furniture

sharp throng pointed
foliage following
swept embankments
        run off and
        away driveways

flesh water ripens
thick green rind
truckload melon
          deep tree pink
          sumac spreading
roots shift
teeth shadows
on arrow reamed
          pointed
          jolt

haunted foliage
lifetime throat
sentence cleared
          bullet
          buttocks
          asking for it
more later all
comes in kissed
          brushed with life
          floor flow stud
          hot with blood
threatening fits
turning over bridge
          stripped creek
          barreled branches

WHO KILLED LAKE ERIE?
WHO KILLED d.a.levy?

oil don't calm
no watered old
can washer rust
burning Cuyahoga

with onions
fish no more
on hamburgered
d.a.levy for sale

City Hall
boat skier
marina powered
skewered plants
crossroad

fish dead
perch carping
lesion lessons:

  Toledo
  Buffalo
  Sandusky
  Cleveland

plastic
waiting
beer bottle
undisposable
indispensable
indisputably gone

  Maumee me
  know how
  to die
  now.

EARLY SETTLERS

corner turn
coming around
  alive sleep
  weary hour
  deep road
  mountain
hearts and
red diamond
surrounded sword
  knees can feel
  clearly see
    city light
    side street
    porches over
    wet pavement
    bus stationed
    queen city square
a better
country that
  pee might
  inhabit
    riverbank
    construction site

five acre rest area
slipped between
fences
fields
forged
too narrow
not wanting sour
soil answers to poor
growing
slender
sparkled
sprinkling
velvet inner
elegant bracelet
mirrored globes
turning bold
light into
emeralds
of hand painted
golden signatures
on unique fingernails

INTO BIRCHES

(for Ron Schreiber, 1934-2004)

catacombed ditches come
into Charles Birchfield
winter tree maple
stub Ohio shrubbery
suburban rain rubbing

Grandmother scenery inside
Black Elk breasts will never
explain binocular headbands
or geometric loneliness
invading rooming houses

without ornament to
undress an opposite harm
in maple green leaves of
skeleton key jailers climbing
interlocked golden ladders

hung over East Fork

willow limb judgment
          in muddy foliage
          watered artery level
          alphabetical currents

louver apple nighttime
seated tree corridor
          pleats clinging
          to missing cue
          climbing gear

floodwall parked
after dark choked
          wrinkled eyes
          quick shooting
          scared shitless

LOUISVILLE ROAD CURVE

fresh twenty-five
year stapled line
car tar approached
cautiously upgrades
motorized transport
radio wireless hanger
transcriptions memorized

will they ever finish
aerial gravy scraping
detour ahead above mud
sparks go by along side
word for word standard shift
stretch hum pickup trucks gone
on down alone into fresh vegetables

past one arc bent
sodium radial lamp
between piled steel
construction workers
in yellow lined sunlight
between shoulders beams
visibility lowered tired

whippet wheel
whisker whittle

whistle whispers
whether wetter or
widespread wing lost
Louisville Road Curve
last exit alibi good-by
location concentrations

    whip why
    when whirl
    whet whine
    white whey
    where what
    whelp whistle
    stormy weather

SCATTERED REMNANTS GRASS REMEMBERS

"Of course
grass does flower"
—Amy Clapett

clustered
pedicel dry
rachis breeze
branched glances
peduncle open mouth
hot sun portico porch
    one sided
    approaching
    two rows spiked
        sheath
        node
        ligules
        midrib
        apex blade
    one reaches another carpet
    stumbling turf web walking
    roots finding wells below
    cellar shared jimmy spurns
    woven threaded treads joined
    thatch shadows spread into
    willows building up showers
    against any shadowed pavement
    circles waiting extended over
    august amber lime tinted lines

maybe pond pool green patched
stitched quilt needle eyes
miss open moss no red stone
unturned toward intrude
sightseers
gather dust
pollen floats
drifting silver
leaves cut
on many horn
blowing straw waved
calm antlers running along
brome with glabrous lemmas
awn tufted erect soft hairy
or nearly smooth membranous
lacerate edged lateral teeth
shallow rooted blunt stiff with
faint parallel nerves glistening
golden or purplish bands all nearer
their diminutive wand-like triple tips

wrinkled circular touched chattered
rough canary red top numerous creeping
rhizome pyramidal rather dense whorled
meadows caught glittering tickle weed wood
barleycorn reed fingered fringe feathered
green foxtail soft slightly nodding out on
ear tip bristled common cornfield and alfalfa
areas alike in undisturbed soil pulled between
teeth picking up silky slick pulp barnyard axis
smoking tall tubes may produce an irritation with
bitter qualities eaten by keeping goldenrod ripens
wheel barefoot domestic astringent medicine chest

colonial burgher
merchant driven
cut down now all
to size for games
lawn mowers row
upon row pouting
about how not to
eat these scarce seed
crows chase away stray
birds taking their pick
and planting them elsewhere

crab grass hero tough sturdy

working class crass dandelions
aren't going to go away from onion's anion
locked back door let in chased away or just
                    saying every day
                    makes its own hay.

WHAT DO TREES DO WHEN ARRANGED WITHOUT COMMAND?

do oak
speak to
oak trees wrestling
                    wind chill
                              thrills
mulberry
lindenwold
          beach
          cedar
          maple grove
                    key winged
                    kinship cattered
                              hard wood
                              carpenter
                              calendar

thesaurus rings
          mahogany
          walnut
          almond
          hickory
          lowly lord
                    crusted locust
                    gusts in pod seeded
                    hedge balls gathered
                              weeping milk

umbrella elm
          cornucopia
          acorn squirrel
          scattered acres
                    pollinating
                    Johnny Applesauce
                              fruit bearing
                              heavy cherry
                                        quince

plumb
peach
seed
pear
white feather
flower festival
shaded lavender
fan dance
torn thorn
food core
a kind of
bow-arrow
twang worn
on cheering
willow
basket
shelter
laurel
dogwood
magnolia
poinsettia
rhododendron
lilac laughter lifted
lazy shade slanted
without hints of pine
rosin redwood Lebanon cedar
groves gathered weeping timber
needles speeding
for departure
eating burning
building paper
pepper milled
on canoes never
forgetting their cargo
words woods
caught in slaughter
open poplar lanes even
land lines scraped where
even those without feet escape

BLACKBERRY THANKS

raw
roar
soft voice lifts off

        upstairs
                chair
                stained

railing
lipping
slips sips
singing head given
        always
        hallway
                doors open
                kissed muscles
                hiss this way
                        and that
                        arrival
                        survival
                        revival

sinks
drinks
links glans to angst
     anus to glass
        tickled
        nipple
        wrinkled clothing
        wrapped around
        snapped ankles
                laughing
                coughs

hovering light
blues drift **away**
        eating angry
        hungry arms
        on feathered
                band
                hand
                stands
gut strung out
        struts
        opens up
        rift valley
        rippled nipple
                upper
                balcony
                alchemy
                becomes gold

green spring
leaves in flower
on railroad bed ties

grow food
against greed
recovered seed
needs given free
vocal unsheltered
shattered steel rail
lesson in every straight ending
carved feeling other curves coming
uncovered

DARK AND BLOODY GROUND

1. FORT ANCIENT

creek blood
fog spread
milk star

streak
throng
silent
congealed

out of breath
highway hill
run away

thick
maple
filled
compost

goldenrod
bones buried
in mounds without
feather traced
serpent genealogy
creeks trees
turn shaggy
across edges over
ancestors
passing by

2. SCENIC VIEW

embered emblem
farmer architect
homespun nut pine
unsheltered Norfolk

and Western track
shell bark sorrow
Little Miami wash
blue black muddy
deciduous trees
in bloody winter
lookout girders

gone one way
highroad under
oak table piecemeal
landlocked footbridges

3. MIRROR LAKE

pink comb
pine needle
Mirror Lake
asleep covered

azalea
magnolia
forsythia
laurel hill

promenade
fire escape
good looking
moist morning

rolled up arm
crimp seated
door handle
rest sticking

Pisces naked
dream shifts
upon a red
bicycle seat

surrenders
open handed
picnic soldier
ground teeth grins
breaking shoulder blades

4. LOCUST TREE

under leaking
locust tan pods
playing rosin skin
        rising
        petiole
        fingers
Goethe counted
divine numbered
children trying
        to smoke them
        keys to Butler
        County Jail House
Greek Revival roof
tornado seeds gone
so far to feel tough
        provisional
        parchment
        bent ripe

stay completely
still and no one
will ever notice

5. AUGUST MOON

sharp zucchini
erect between
corn hoe rows
shod pumpkin
moon unfolds
zipper stone
cut green grass

picas hiss cellulose
warm silk roads
so narrow
flesh curls

before beggars
can pass going down

singing
cornered
feathers
double-timing
just to say hello

6. GROUNDSWELL

cold damp night
grass different
feeling distant
stranded noisy
in Levi traffic

sleeping saddled
tractor-trailer
Kessler downed
island hidden
cricket crow
silk throat

sharp ditch silver clearing
unbuckled acorn jeans on back seat
wrinkled turnpike exit navy cans eat
beans under side road culvert exits

STONELICK CREEK BED

I. SPRING PLOWING

shiny bladed
silver steel
layers cut
intoxicated
language turns

crawl worm
black loam
fresh smell
sunlight so
smooth faced

new plow
furrow felt
confused odor
revealing spilt
north winds spitting

II. SUMMERTIME MARIGOLD

marigolden
truer bloom
blown tufted
cracked acrid
flame columned
sterno needling
quicker dissolution

repelling
blood mood
stung insect
yellow petaled
acrobat heaven's
pants come apart
in back circled leaves of
        crushed crockery
        flower scenery

III. BUTLER COUNTY FAIR

green tomato
morning star
midway quilt
pickled scrap
relished corn

watermelon
rind spread
with dahlia
daisy sulky
axle greased

ferris wheel
merry-go-round
trotter racing

after dry fodder
smelling fresh clover

shouting absolute
alfalfa in sawdust thunder

IV. HEDGEBALLS

hedge rows gone
wild weed wood
hides away in
OWensville

corncrib barn
abandoned hen
house stripped
branch water body

ball thrown
slippery creek
wet flesh green
tree milk tastes

batter upper
bitter potato
tight lip patched
old games of chance

V. EAST FORK

grapevine tendril
water skin fruit
arm handled raw
sunshine field
pants dripping

swimmers swing
face dangerous
out from shore
underwater fore
shortening splashes

sing laugh ready to go
into backstroke melodies

VI. BLACKBERRIES

fresh spaced flesh
wet filled blackberry
tender shining texture
fruit smiles face
where abandoned
farms drop from
wooden frames

rusty paint
locust tree
fence wedding
full moon grown
wild grapes and
poison ivy webbed
inside lattice bedded

sassafras trees
no joke horse sense
to a child serious
as a railroad track

UNRETURNABLE

interior log
built before
split paneled
        wood worked
        double jointed

back road shack
splendor out of
right away rail
        driven hands
        splitting hair

pocketed attachments
hidden in pursuing
industrial waste
        broken in
        two places

deep woods
trees stand

against Miami's
come home attack
un-feathered skylight

purple along Plum
Street shaded fountain
drinking to drive home
        alone is to make
        love in hiding

spring song canteen
winding road thrown
rod thruway lost
        passage lists
        unknowable words

in trade winds unspoken
spinning traffic island
ball bearings jump ship
        start running away
        is only a beginning

PERFECTION PEAKS

monumental filled
violet smothered
green grass hill
        setting sun
        observatory

let loose Eden
Museum flowered
musical garden
        white boys
        doing it here

on layered lawn
hair open spread blooms
electrical towers
        thrown away
        lost pieces

gathered on
Taft circle
winding uphill

spring roots
all ready to go

search attack
catch running
water spigot
mouth stem
cream stream

colored buds bursting
heading west after
a good meal
wheels whirl
weave golden handed

tipped tongue nips
pull off clothes
from downhill settlers
where every wind
blows new seed

UNFIXED WAYS

fond hope
impatience
chrysanthemum
overworked
lawn future
furniture lost

lookout train
crossing trellis
into tonight
teeth watch
golden plated
yards switching

armored
and hardly
dangerous
gone over
head driven
locomotives

for food
will work

bronze door
    figured
    fountain
    square mounted

one room
schoolyard
pickup picture
    comforter
    pulse piece
    painted one eye

half acre
road hidden
down and out
    side cedar
    ladder lath
    chipped pattern

part glued
grain alcohol
sandpaper matched
    in fire's late
    way of advancing
    gravel propinquity

DAYTON ASYLUM

town movie pass
ping pong rubber
hilltop gray wire
cupola diner lined
cement stained railing

red hour paddled
denim legs signed
going onto fifteen
fifty meshed feeling
Wayne with table love

arisen fresh surprising
tied up minds holding
once a week friendly
obstinate run-away
wing fence doctor
gone on syphilis

playing free time
all alone old record
backup light corridor
visitor screams park in
director's reserved signed

lot space easily seen
except how to get out

FLOWERING KALE

flowering kale
finds another
winter once
without food
shoes
dishes

of bed words
recovering
rediscovered
uncovered rest

fitting
filling
flitted
filtering

more comfortable in
Potown running
on a ruby dog
playing dead
pointed swan
processional
inside gravel
rose tinted curls

IF THEY RUN ME OUT OF OHIO

waterway waves
cross over bus routes

too many things run
broken connections

now head through
don't go normal

money talk
transfers

everything dark green
night motion drugged
fear shooting gravy
water pans expand

another
monster

scrambled egg bread
sliced tomato cob
bean potato corn
salt-pork cabbage

brother
cartilage

dog laughter knows
already why smell
after explosion
leg gaps break

take
a leak

corridor nut door
wallboard payment
cautions comfort
some day soon

clone splice
well seeded
reserved

laundry money
Uncle Ed
mud

cinnamon sugar
red tomato
preserves

concord grape
strained
juice

starved alone
no one ever
hungry

feedbag dress
for musical
clothing

chicken yard
corn picked
frying

saddle basket
bushel peck
measure

Mildred skin
curled toe
marriage

school planned
escape exit
husband

fodder field
fence lane
clover

says "don't
sass back
ugly bitch"

soul murdered sisters
in front yard
house

carpenter barn
back lot
cellar

cider pie
mason jar

jam

another word
mother has
for it

SUMMER TIME

thigh oh
so high
corn sky
        tasseled
        vessel

seed weed
by another hand
        name
        same
        pleasure
leisure
time goes
on running
        away
        threaded

thorn needles
left over worn
        finger
        ring sings
        singed

hot summer
sun festival
        carnival
        circus animals
                alive

with fire
lightning
strikes twice
        as fast
        as lime time
thimbles tremble
lost in hiding
        under roofs
        over rocks

day and night
two faces one
        wish
        to be
        elsewhere

another side
lane path road
        overgrown
        sassafras
        grape arbor

fruit bears
sweet laden
harmony spheres
        vibrate
        liberate
        celebration

ERIE CANAL HIGHWAY

enamel refrigerator
necessary laughter
Daddy never spoke
peanut hull floor
dry shells eaten

scrap part lot
tree lined alley
Erie canal filled
White City Auto Sale
zinc tub nut chrome trim

radio vent aerial
clutch choke gears
harness strap brace
brake steel shoe toe
distributor cap fuel
pump carburetor shield
lamp handle ring valves
walking cinders through

cylinder block
sedan horn shade
condenser cushion
points fender shaft

joint drop bolt lock
stock water bolt condenser
spark steep pitched horseshoes

used they want
your throat out
heart weeds stop
commerce grown up
men dye one another
underneath shades of
unseen '55 automobiles

haunch tough north wind
hisses inside maple foliage

BARBED WIRE

daisy garden
backdoor porch
ice cream suited
truck knife ringed
barbed wire splitting

cone trapezoid
cornfield razor
bush elderberry
clod house feast
thirsty trapped row

not until ending
lime green ring
lacquered cedar
red barn door
copper hinged
clasped hook

edges mitered sealed
mulberry oak maple
gray velvet gold
fringed widowed
tonsils on wing

root sunk mauve
willow swelling
green wood branch

soil turned brown
bent sapling trunk

crowded table legend
fried frog legs moved
across Fort Anthony Wayne
empires smiling to expire
    wet sweat pond
    water near blue
    green wet algae
    frond throat
    slime grass
    thick root
    twitching
    tendriled
white tablecloth
talks silverware
belt buckle gone
    away to war
    playing wagon
    wheels in season
    beyond all reason

IN OBLIVION OHIO

supremely
simple details
    lost in
    higher
    decibels

undecipherable
hum speech only
    heard by flying
    tree insects

mochis bitten
in driving rain
    fatigue
    following
    Jose Marti

Madonna
cell phone
has nothing

        to say
        walking

by in
crested cable
        car to
        iron oar
        mountain

goat
throat
begins to
        swim
        singing

of cloud
fibers lost
on brick rock
thick upper lips
        departing

voices over
shadow clouds
under toe trough
        wild
        cacti

act their
own age leg
cathedrals grow up
on sliding hillside
descent into purple oblivion.

AT LONG LAST LAUGHING

need new
clay some
way to say
        what was
        not lost or
tossed away
architectural
broken in shoe
        accidental
        actuality

Queen Anne's
hidden lace
    crevice
    crack culvert
    concentrated in
musical
sneezing
a way through
    outdoor
    concerts
adored
indoor
dimples
    turned simple
    as a head spin
double
gainer

nothing ever
    lost or
    found alone
late better
than never
waiting
    wading for fronds
    to step twice
    into a shoe
shod horse
toothed whinny
always a winner
never shines alone
    in Afton
where dishes
go around washing
    machine
    empty well
        bucket
still water disaster
only a quarter hour
    away
    gone on to
    sunflower seed

WELL MET ON PARKAMO

has they ever
yet met Audrey
before voice
rink linked

sharp tongue
yowl moan sob
used to be
hard to get
there to wang
wail whelp
bawl yell
holler into
crying out
loud far
enough for
lands' sake
taken sides
shook
stones letting loose

skip work wrap
around kin come
fifty miles wanted
it real bad wired
up to get by most
folks weird
hear
tell dry
turnip
hell
sooner
freeze
over
pumpkin
pie stuck
up pins
all ass backward

angels don't let
on they'll leave
until

good and

ready when
sung before
winder ledges will just

as leif fly

TIME BROKEN HANDS

"arise shining martyrs" - John Wieners

BURNT

NOTHING BEHIND THEM

"One priest told me we were savages, that we had no traditions, no civilization, that we were merely responsive to the hollow sound of words, without putting ideas behind them."

—Leopold Sedar Senghor

hollow sound
        stick
        stomach
                machinery
                        chin
                        china
                        chatter
                        later clatter
masks
mated
matter
splatters
unmated
all molten
eaten alive
unsweetened
street sounds
fooling around
        pounded level
        ground
        surrounding
        circumstantial
                foot feet floors
                meeting head on
                        hard
                        horny
                        heavy
unsteady to a
greedy beat growl
                grown into
                gravel voiced
                choice pearled
                        fist
                        foist
                        moist
tears then drop
topping it all off
hopping along alone

        unnumbered
                slumbering
                        unencumbered by

messages
massaged reach
        each lumbar
                spinal chord
                regional
                        sword tap
                                lap
                                lip
swift spit
        split
        shift
                mood needs no
                move over or ever
                more before stopping

CLUTCH

"It will break the clutch." H.D.

clutch broken
        bitten
        bitter
        bridle leather strap
                smooth trap
                patch worn.
                bracelet ankle
catch
watch
latch
patch
hatch
match gear to gear
        wheel to wheel
        girl to girl
        boy to boy
        pearl to pearl
        joy to joy each grasp
                        let go gallop
                        grab laughter
                        disasters flattered
                                shattered

friction
fiction
diction of all's well
wound up
with wounds
of wanting whips
when lips kiss too sweet
for words
afford no
relief sleep
dream exits
silk skin
rubs hands
together in
storage boxes
aroused tan
glands glad
clutches
splintered
hardwood
benchmark
beaten into swollen feet
Argive sandals
survive too much
attention takes time

LIME QUARRY

"My mind has gone to seed."

mind seed
rag weed in ditches
between rusted
car parts sidewalks
backyard unguarded
approaches without looking
sign of
bad soil
or none at all
growth against
rules elimination
killer formulas laboratory
experimental
herbicide
twinges yellow
faded messages

                              massage getting
                              thru cracks
white thin
roots state
          highway cutter
          scythe blade
          sharp level stroke
          hot sun enough
          to fry an egg remains
                    ground level
                    wilting head dress
                    waiting for Judy Garland
                              her come back
rough lace
green slivered
coarse cloth
          see through
          quilted stockings
                    rattlesnake
                    stroke flower
                    storage sneezes
                    pollen participation
                              precipitation
everything
fringed frayed
finger winged
silver beyond lime
layered alphabet of direct
          sunlight
          survival

ROME WAS BUILT IN ONE DAY

“Room is all we have now”

no more quick
step dances creak
bones stirred from
Stanley shoe
foot dance only
two moves before
          everyone goes
          loose into sound
          waves unrecorded
                    don’t say dough
                    and allemande left

Pennsylvania
farmers square
dance fairy
furbelowed Tanya
        asks for French
        Fries in Dutch
        Country no one
        turned into cornbread
                for wearing
                down teeth
reach for
another hand
quietly tent
lent camouflage
        flap flange
        russet hair
        between teeth
        so stone so
        quick will
        be back to
                leaves change
                shades directions
                places where turnips
                        split pea stew
                        iron pot cooking
retains carbon
trace forever
in sparkling
mouths lips
maple maybe
what will never be
        known were
        wilted sobs of joy

WOODEN STRUCTURE

okra climb
rhyme line
slime skin
        sideways
        to always

heart vein
stamp weed
seed bleeding

strong heart
blood root

change rings
roots milk
ink writes
moving hand
cream pods

heat come
hear home
fires frying
onions
on ladders

crow stem
beak sun
windows shine
warmer
in winter

wait tent
wet trees
try now turning
over under
thimble blankets

face tom
wing basket
tree thatched
for every
season affection

crestfallen
reason reckons
cross fingers
better now
than ever

JEWELS OF EXPLORATION EXPLOITATION

C'est la vie
they die in
innocent thirty
what percentage
how many years

appeal doubts
libels trials
eventually executed
cut off
course of
burnt labels
reading glass
magnification
dezincification
functional
people who didn't
do anything
mistake in every system
overcrowded cells
repeat offenders
uncertainties
punishment
banishment

standing still
dead no name
slippage glass
crushed sharp
edges flattened
faultless wooden
absolute mercy faucets

turned off
floods floors
upper stories
without La Jolla aloe

swift judgment
tournament of
eccentricities after
incomplete adornment

jewels
journeys
whistle and
watch those teeth
no one leaves here alive

CARLO CAFIERO

"haunted by the thought that the windows of his room might be giving him more than his just share of sunlight."

Woodcock, Anarchism

squint
shade
roped
spring
locked
in glass embrace
        membranes
        unexplained
        embarrassment of riches
                too much given
                thrown away
                taken down
                forgotten
beamed into
some remote
eye controlled
        rainbow distance
        measured cup
                pound
                inch
                saucer
                caution
treadmill
machinery
staples reminders
        debts unforgiving
        deaths with every
                breath
mirrors
refuse
any king
parliament
potted silver clasped
        orange trees
        space taken
        up next charged
                lodges
                against seeing
                                sun shine
caught

watching
wallowing
in golden hands
too narrow
to correct
    completely invisible
    concrete attachments

WEDDING BELLS RINGING WEEDS

pleasure tax
gaming card
royal seal
charge born
other end of
town Tom Hill
served out his
apprenticeship to
a playing card maker
    aces queens
    deuces kings
    knaves and staves
    coins and trumpets
He went to Holland
to have a die made
in order to be able
to counterfeit England's
    duty stamp
    paid from
    beginning
    to last call
    dice thrown against

purple felt inspectors
        informers
        infiltrators

hanged
for this
post mortem revival
    cold February
    Seventeen forty
    three old style
    new style brings
    blood to spring
    frozen from veins

circulation stopped
re-stopped breath windpipe
choked on
rope so
young so
broke full
of hope fallen
Druid's groan
into their number
dropped deck cardboard
design on Tybum field
apple sellers eat their fill
counted out in fifty-two's
too new to
know *He was cut*
down and carried
by mistake to
Benjamin's surgeon
Jack Jock
groom wound
worm ring
wearer bearer
bell ringer
fit to be tied
dressed to kill
says I will always
comeback to haunt
you cadaver of delight
Aces of Hearts/Spades embraced.

ESPRIT SEGUIER

aged skin
shiver
shriveled eyelid
given visions

my soul is a garden
of shade and fountains

waterworks
sprays displays
light flickers
fingernails
handrails

herbs culinary
medicinal
vines in
rows of
shrubbery
poplar series
of marigolden.
bell tower blown
closed flowers
colors against
horseshoe
mud prints
leaving behind
eaten cabbage
patched on both
sides' bourgeoisie
court stenographers
collecting pieces of
conversation published
perished
persistence
writing arm
instrument

a Frenchman doesn't wave
his arms... all the time.
Sometimes he waves them in
one way and sometimes in
another—and sometimes, I think,
he stops waving them. (Bateson)

flack
flap
flag
flax
flaw
flay
flat
flab
flaccid
flavor
flame
flare
severed joint
small carpal bones

split
spit

he tore it the rest
of the way off with
his teeth.

Peasants of Languedoc, p. 283

Gregory Bateston,
"Metalogue, Why Do Frenchmen?"
Steps to an Ecology of the Mind

INSIDE WARSAW

some drank
sewer water
and died
others waited
voice need
less point
dropped rock
echoes unable
to get out
just lists
teachers
aids to
remember
bomb
raids
kings
reigns
rumors start present events
circle back
deep well re-
lay
lax
relations

re traced
frain
train
playing
afraid to
sleep

ex-
plosive
pensive
tract
ex
pletive
pect
trict
pend
a little
light bird
sings shrill
young face was all
everything
to go on
broken
boundary
operations
mending can never

re open
pair
place
lieve
apply
appear
position
anything but
relive only
historians mop
up blood so thick
smelling of their

ab-sence
solute
stract
negation

ablative
abrogate
abomination

ob- stinate
stuctive
solete
ob- stacle
servation

obsessions putting numbers
on strings
changed to
chain over
night bro-
ken one
way no
entry

anachronism
chronology
ontology
onus anus
exploding

JAZZ

COLORING

skin peeled
pen writing
on rubbing
alcohol sun
eye level shade
drawn crayons
scraped off

flakes calm clam
just when you
didn't expect
messages come

yellow green
blue mint to
harmony part
pastel basic
round edge
faded peg
square space

angry townspeople
country travelers
blinds singed who
only wanted to talk

silver chrome
bright rainbow
burns a circle
around those
hard nipples
anger revenge
Moloch flames

painted city
walls break
tinted glass
fire escape

to where pigmentation
runs open onto free streets

SHOULDN'T HAFTA CRY

  violin incense
  smoke oh my gosh
    trumpet finger
    valve two three
swing horn
half daddy
  piano nimble
  cymbal sharks
bluff hand
cuffs stud
  pearl clarinet
  blind flirt
drum headed
dumb call another
  drink
  think
  you see saxophone
    calls walls
    broken cold
    water room
Freddie rumble
after all you make
tea sleep alright
  wait a minute
    uptight
    trombone
    sends good looks
    rambling mind
  twinkle feet
  fast seruns
  broken in two
    time step
    three to waltz
      hugging
       ig ng
      Jtggmg
      jiggling along
  away lonely
  moan fat lip
    fat ass
    fat face
    fathead
fat fatter

pass blue
quick gay giggle

bridge
what would you
do without
used to be

APROPOS CHARLIE GREEN

"Charlie Green... became prey of the Depression and was found frozen on the doorsteps of a Harlem tenement"

—liner note to *Empty Bed Blues*

Amsterdam am
let cold bottle
blanket wet blue
doorstep room
landing stops
frost snow stoops
slow bothered gin
dream right here
steal somewhere
runs off pork
fat beat cut in
get in get out
there rich folk
champagne dream
avenue green lip
brickbottom daddy
run away bucks
skin cold two times
calling momma home
sweet honey chance
Dutch sour window
fox without hole
dead and mean mud
treated sheep dog
sniffing dope nose
funnel fun funny
running drip drift
go to hell ground
tell Lou Lou drops
in sometime show
no place to go
ice mattress

EVERYTHING WORKS

was queens listened
eyes wet
Atlantic House
iny man's gone
gravy stains
sailor suits
me fine and
then cracked
skull fracture
face pulped
ditty
piss elegant
me rich they
say buying rounds
everything sounds
so good and
drunk falling
over back alleys
crying
playing cards
beer bottle
pissing piano
blood splintered
glass shattered
dreams of being
a star feature
they'll crawl crayons
draw onions
outback
on top
licking ego
diffused
refused
confused
different
fear
faint
painted eye watches
patches of
flexible veins
search direction
everything
spread out
in oblivion whispers

even more
scorn than
sought just
a mansion or
new mercury speed
tracks in mud

escapes a
melody
searches
for he
won't let
go jokes

about queers
knows safe
here needle
parking lot where
exit corridors
reverberate
verb sticking
absurd snap
trap
table folded
inside is a
message:

you get angry
you get killed
you don't get angry
you kill yourself

self pity
is a city
peopled with
red velveteen
wallpapers
oversized lamps
purple cosmetics
run always
in tears set to go off
on Sunday gas
bills pills pillows
bullets razor thin
edges enough to get
ready for laundry
on Monday

lines begin
again satin
assembly
shopping for
pitchfork
smiles of owners
growing "everything
works for us"
under their belt
yield corridors of
lazy afternoons
without silver
service they desire
they expire
die

BLACKBERRY THANKS

raw
roar
soft lift off voice
upstairs
stains
chairs
railing
lipping
lapping
flipping
sip slipping
singing head given
always
hallways
doors open
muscles kiss
hiss this way
arrival
survival
revival
sinks
drinks
links glans to anus
anus to glans
tickle
nipples
wrinkles clothing

wrap around
ankle
snap
laugh
cough
a light hovers
blμes drifting away
eating angry
hungry army
for feathers
band
hand
stand
gut string
strut
open up
rift ripple
upper
balcony
alchemy
gold becomes
green spring
flowers lay
in railroad beds
grow food
from greed
recovered seed
need given
vocal shelter
steel rails shattered
every straight ending
carved to feel other curves coming
uncovered

FOR EUBIE BLAKE (1883-1983)

"None of them made it
but me… So maybe
I'm making up for them."
—Eubie Blake.

loss of will
dropped into
oblivion soft

scented tea
spoon needle
mantle piecing

2

pierced
murder crush
brain express
train tied down
tight wire cutter

3

childbirth hurt
inflammation in
fection fecundity
severed connections

4

war casualty
delivered with
out means of
entry enlistment
cancelled quickly

5

embroiled argument
groundless quarrel
ends unresolved
unraveled completely

6

open field play
every wild loose
disguised grain
of hate opened
fatal terminal

7

mother another
hard road to

follow getaway
scattered kids

8

invasions
injections
epidemics

9

battleground
musical chord
pulled ligament
laughter caught

10

lost trying
husband mean
religious water
heartless attack

11

piano implantations
escaped plantation crop
groaning grin gift lifted
into a chariot swinging
low sweet delivery
messenger of all who
failed to escape sharp edges

OARS

VOICING MORTAR MOTOR

sometimes
they don't listen
        verbal mouth
        voice force face
        forward gesture
        words come outside
and play
eat clay
sand day
mud pie sky
        porch roof
        broadcast ear
        twisted into eye
        because it was
        easier to say get away
lack of
a sharp
instrument
flat surface
        floss
        choice
        rejoice
        rejoin sentences
                        come in terms
                        of how well
                        armed you are
my sunshine
singing bindery
bugle grinding
        past
        blast
        fast exhaust pipe
                      gripe
                      swipe
                      wipe
                      ripe
spit spat spate
across magistrate's
judgment seat
        Zeon of Eleus
        to Demylous ruler
        edge sharpened
                tongue Anaxarchus
                of Abdera bit off

spat bloody enfaced
tyrant Nicocreon
crushed while still
alive in one last word

JINGLE JANGLE

all together
now one
now two
now three
unto nth power
come Carmen
Carmen Jones
Carmen Miranda
Beatles Brahms
twelve string banjo
fiddle roofing cat
tin pan alley Allen
Joplin
Lady Sings
cold storage cocaine
A Train to D Train
Bartok microcosms
Chopin washing
dishes mercy
motor town house
explosion which
way wind blow
John Coltrane
Love Supreme
Ravi Shankar
pearl inlaid rose
zither hill calling
me home vaudeville
Mudsville
Golden sequin
Judy Garland
Anton
Amadeus
Stravinsky
mullein and bumblebee
gardens of Lido gamin
lures old show tunes country
and western

Andalusian
ballads Lorca
gypsy fireside

flamingo
guitar heavy
rock stable
beaten drum
head Hendrix
Janice Hard
raining metal
Big Band
a cappella
Gregorian chants
tonsured monks jerk
off AC/DC Blondie
Madonna
Ultimate Spinach
Zappa Dead
Kennedys Crass
Clash
Crash
Cash

and carry
whatever can
carry a tune
purse soon
loon songs
lute flue
flute choices are
an absence of voices

RENO MOTEL

stamp lamp
vamp camp
tramp scamp
ramp cramp
double postage
half-acre portage
scraped reportage
strap
crap
trap
wrap

scrap
perhaps
scrape grape
blue green
shoulder gloves
wanted to
get out of
what dust
too close
often closed
door handle
knuckle jam
nipple pincher
wire
pliers
applicationary
over and ten
times twelve above
all else leave
something unturned
stone catches feathers
making
faces beats
wet pillow
debt follows
groves cut by
diamonds too big
to swallow
without water
everything becomes Nevada

GNOSIS

inside Antietam
driveway bridges
overtime cards
shuffling along
way from home
front centuries
avoid walls take
sides slices of
pie cake pan
horse drawn crayon
Kenny's penis
Constitution of

Athens Greek Letter
call boy soldier going
down furnished
room cedar chapel
about to be stuck
pig pork poke
corn horn porn
bend born break
water on rocks
get getter guest
go gutter west
whoa worn vest
gnosis shine
cordovan butt
against northern winter
southern moss
when we arrive
we have yet to
leave tips remember
working for a
living's no joke
six foot above
six foot under
touch your
toes in order
to flow
fly

JUST SPIT IT OUT

throat
goat
groan oat
eat
earthen
guttural
sphincter
wind
send
gym
bend
lend
grin pipe
pip
slip

ripe
reap
grip
grime
swing
back roof
jackknife
dive drive
alive lateral
literal spit
split letters
word salads
ballads sad
lads lifting
tongues trap
dispatch grasp
raspy
Ralph
raspberry
jelly belly
laugh comes
up valve
work slurp
surf teeth edge
wedge
hedge
badge beaten
tinny
tummy
tunnel lungs
lunge
plunge
carburetor
mixture air
gasoline ignite
red blood
red head
hothead
watch cock
disc ditch
dip stick
monostitsch
switched rod
traffic comes
before construction
workers are satellites

between stalactites and
stalagmites

DIAMOND SPARKS

dismissal
rehearsal
bicycle turbine
fan mulch
tum over
outgrowth
inside looking
hard hot issue
tissue thin
golden piss
caught light
melted steaming
messages inscribed
in molting
snow slide
mountain
side show
menstruation
monuments
ground into gravel
travel
sand thrown
into wind
funnels castles
U tum tunnels
cycles
caught cluck
clutch
clack
clatch
cleat
clean
couch
clock only
prefigures
never delivers
shivers sentences
follow irregular
patches paths
pants patterns

double stitched
nothing gets
out without asking
to go party
stop parking

EXORBITANT DEMANDS

articulation
so simple
as hanging sings
hand painted
Franklin stove recalled
redundancy elimination
first extra
then all words
letters syllables
go leaving only
ideogram icon

hanging
shingles
follow nerve
ends soaking
burning up
cells destroyed
virus retreated
outside stream of traffic
who sees spells
what sells well
by design more
come in cob web
which needs to know
signals original arrivals

bells
harnesses
saddles black
felt cowboy hat
number twelve
jersey identification
never reaches identity

every rest
stop brings

another discussion
please dont argue
tonight tomorrow
will not necessarily
be another day marked
by body armor amour

pours out
by heart
some familiar
story big front
little interior
wizard of
tin cans each
carry several
labels libels
secret code written in
machinery manufacturer's
date of entry
shelf life stele
from ancient Argos

Argonauts
claimed they
could recognize
alchemists by
chemical cymbals
ringing from a cave
fallen in cones carving
what is ignored
becomes absorbed
by deep fleece towels
drapes
floor mats

either say
welcome or
give a random number
or are completely silent
fully absorbent
flooding reversal
Please Wipe Your Feet Before Entering

POLISH POLIS POLANDISH POLONAISE

sign paint
putty print
   cans brushes
   liquid spectrum
   pyramid split
   light waves hello
         purple pale
         green lime
         red blue
         yellow pea
         coat orange
         peach cream
         brown pink
         black coffee
         mocha almond
tattoo body
ready to work
risen erect
early morning
   reversal
   stand up and
   be counted Prague
   street numbers names
   rubbed raw removed
   deliveries delayed maps
by counting
steps remembering
circulation each
gate opening you
get around Labrador
      El Salvador
         stalemate
         statement
         read from chain
         lettered hotel lobbies
drawn lines
circles designs
pictorial hinges
wherein hangs
a first story
   when books
   go incognito
   loose their
   money given

titles holding
securities accounts
windows receivable
discretionary visibility

VOICE CHOICE

motorcycle
voice recital·
river bend bed
    whirl **wind**
    liquid vapor
    lockfook
    before crossing
    or dotting teeth
cap force
feet crown
post ghosts filter flats
    low lands
    larynx lynx
    eyed obelisk
    risk free obsidian
tether
totter
roller
skater
    gnosis nose
    Texas rose
    nobiscus close
    proboscis clothes
    Gibraltar rock
        halter
        falter
        shelter powder
            powered
            pollen count
            down shore
shout
shot
short
shining path
sucking water
bubbling brook
        brake
        breath art

tart
fart
cart
part
start
quarter
guardian
monitor
mountain
tonsils anima
stamina

EXILE

Exile is so
slow wheels
caught wings
going growing
baggage hats
hands heavy
wateIWays sailing into
still seas
stormy weather
wind tacking cloth
liquid internal combustion
knives forks
metal teapot
china cups saucers
road show
success load
unload rehearse
until once after
that every performance
anti climax
so much more
to forget
feet crossed
stool seated
standing room
only tourist
class staring
directly ahead
goes nowhere
in particular
where are you from

where do you work
what are you doing here
detective
conversation
turns up enough
holes to crawl in
hanging around until
cloning closing time
last call begins to tell
bells following folding chairs
wrapped in arm
length hatcheck
can always handle
another big tip

all other avenues
are closed

GLOSSINDOS

PINK POTATO

1

medallioned mansard
filled drawers coat
hangers and exlax
hung heavenly true
fruit flavor closet
floor toppled salt
taffy man coming

2

seldom seen forest
queen known done
bleeding fictions
pike's peak bust
top inlaid teak
sailors eat hair
foreign words weeds

3

buffalo campfire girls
go out alone tonight

GRAPE ARCHITECTURE

All surroundings are
referred to high water
until some alabaster
continent freed in red suited
joggers between traffic islands
florescent honey suckle
instead of hard details
reinforced umbrella enamel
in stone ground grillwork
        crocheted
        grapes tum
        earrings plaid
        eyes playing
        brown bag ideas
        so close to laughter
        geraniums become

        motors in air pockets
mind keep out of this
hard turn poplar vines
sodium speed light life
long suffering clutch
slipping adjectives added
        to raining manikin
        purple wardrobes
        in diamond basins
        boats embark bent
        handles waving every
        part of speech goodbye
grey Lady of Vapors frown
on shore no one is a safe

        carnivorous fish
        swim between
        ice water flats
        and boiling vats

icon transfer leaves
cold limestone bone
ivory playing cartilage
hiss icepack Artemis
length narrow cheeks
eat trouble enough
making ends meet
        this circle
        silence asylum
        starter warning
        trunk lid
        siren sleep
        spoiled wheeling
architect fashioned shoulders
to bear boys returning flavors
to where they were on Ipswich Street
        copper statuary
        padlocked flagpole
        exhibitors enter
        deep throats of
        imitation glamour
shoe laced Middlesex
hotel lobby police
pickpocket heavy
luggage filled teeth
last minute survivals

no burnt fuses or
busted hot water heaters
phone disconnected
electricity and gas
shut off delinquent
mint green slit white
shirt shoe tufted hair
high heel leisurewear
dance music cocktail
leftover fresh eels
in ashtray sequined cookies

Oh my tired feet
we've walked all day
I just wanta
take a hot bath

SILENT EMBROIDERY

silent embroidery
sewn in pewter
slashed blue
woven red lace
idle filigrees
hang part frilled
with light bulb
blanket dog groans
pastel paddled
bubble balloons
rainbow spectrum
freeing Duer birds
thrown into flight
angel star
apocalyptic
bishop vision
dusty bridge
reddened eye
bitten bottom
with purple apples

FRUIT STAIN STRAINS

gold lame vines
marbled paper

green birds in
purple racks
white vulture
baby parrot
papyrus rose
Cyrus stem
Mughal shah
plaited blade
pilot hairs on
orange sparrow
experiences
cosmos chrys-
anthemum belt
buckle seed
cedar arrow
yellow curlew
blue whisper
fire displays
jewelry feathers
jade knives
ivory animals
spawn unseen
peacock marl
crying acrid
elephant sweet
thin flying
Palmyra fig
caught inside
honey cake
matted pond lily.
smocked perfume
luted lovers
worship lip
sacred lingam
sparkled courtly
square counted
house garden
monkeys sons
princesses cough
out a landscape
hunting miniature
palace flowers
bunched abed
ancient lei liege
lady in chains

        aching ribs
        giant painting
        flame tree
crones arise in pointed majesty

TAKEN AND FORGOTTEN

nature
        turning
        Nathaniel
        Southampton
                catch a life
                get busted
                seeing blood too soon
of adjectival poems
        attributes
        attributions
        flying singing buttresses
                guts
                guys
                dolls
human import
        deportment
        unemployment
        deportation
                skin
                skip
                slip out of
party pantry
        pleasant enough
        said and done took
        overlook scenic view
                without ink
                        link
                        leak
to be radical
        redial
        labial spoke
                clock
                choke
                        stress
                        radius
                        arrested
movement
monument
momentary

Governor
Wise vice versa
nice persons never finish
words escaped lips
collapsed signal
rehearsal
ship
shift
surprise arrival

OLD RECORDS

scratches
itches inches
sounds stumble
crumble
mumble gargling
gangling
gobbling
gurgling
gable
gamble
gagging
grumbling
Demosthenes
gathered sea
gravel shells
resonate
insensate
aggravate
aggregate
decognate
congregate
conjugate water
rubbery
cock spring
thing
ringing soft
lubrication

vibration
pea weed
pod wise
purposeful
problematic

mouthful
doubtful
dreadful transmission
        slippage
        drifting away choke
            cough
            clutch
            crutch of ages
                  timing whacked
                  off internal
                        eternal law
                        of thermodynamics packaged

combustion
exhaustion
congestion
suggestion
lesson intake
injection
slippery belt

      stones caught
      unawares turn
      down another fence red
            row
            raw
            rough
            running
riding half tuned
carburetors fuel
cruel injections
      objections
      inspections
      interjections leave starved
            scales
            scorn
            scarves
            scars
            stars
cold starting
is never easy

BROKEN FINGERS OF TIME

you cant buy time
      glitter express

coffee jars
brass spit tune
ass candles
burning both ends
spending doing cheating
metronome
chrome   just
so many miles
per hour revolutions
per minute beats percolations
record guess opinion questions

wishes
and who is on
third base soccer
jersey wine famous
for grapes which
grow in used car hubcaps
antique mustang
stopping everyone
wound up vintage year
different calendars
celebrations
calibrations

split level
underground
garret high overhead
under intoxication
midtown fumes gasoline
drink kerosene acetone
airplane wings held together
suddenly Thomas Jefferson
surrenders Tripoli to hashish
airplane trip
explains Hindenburg
lead landing
on Pittsburgh
Williamsburg
golden watches
Just drop down play
big battery amps mixers
and it can all be as temporary
or as permanent as I want it to be

Time is money

only as long
as Jose doesnt
run away with
book keeping
for blood letting
go only binds tighter

Domesticity and all that isn't forever

(Jimmy Page quotations)

ORCHARD ANCHORS

cloverleaves
dug in Belgian
cheeses and ripe
cherries so long
trees to bear neighbors
breaking limbs
birds arriving
early warm cerise
juice burning news
gas station
Levi leather
belt tattoo
back seat
ass muscle
handle bar
bent mouth
warm oilskin
twenty four hour
loading dock who
could know in
Nineteen Fourteen
collect call of un
raveled pouches
deposited whirlwind
tour which never went back
middle class
peace comes
donuts do
get stale
or go away
in lard vats
swimming for

survival of
anything bridged
comes unhinged
by passage twisted

misplaced
points broken
limbs boulders
crushed stone
entering guardians
transferred layers laminated
impacted wishes
shifted generations
don't you resemble
your grandmother's smile?

NO REST REST STOP

stainless
steel wall
door undressed
mirror
image lips
fingers pearl
of Antilles facing
out to another
ivory ocean
gold chain
charm bracelet
whisper breath
swelling fogging
up Narcissus
swim
suit
down
town
boy next
door opens.
flocked hair
pubic public
urinal arrival
flash
flush
flesh
pulled out

pulled off
groan get
off and running
water sink
saddle purple
maximum face
to face with doing
it again and
again every
time a bus stops
a pickup
and get it out
Yucatanic

SURRENDER

run Toto
run into
out of
off schedule
turn
tune
tunnel
total break
brink
brittle
brilliant
hearty
sprout
spouts
springs
sprinkle
sparkle
overtime
nine dime
incline ten seconds
shirt un
buttoned
everything
askew
blue sweet
sweep
swelling stone
stairway to
heaven is where
we inherit sandals

ringing
hand bells
foot wells
cells tell nothing
    about tangled
    escarpments escape
        get out
        get off
        get wet
        getaway
        to Prague

GREEN FIELDS LAUGHING

pearly gates
e lephants' trunks
animals incinerated
    tough hides
    keyboards
    fingers float
grandmother's wedding
    gift enameled
    packages soap
    pelfumes every
    idle luxury saved
brushed blue
denim cotton
wrinkled hair
    hillsides walk
    gardens exotic
    delicate filigree
    foliage can't
    wait to see flowers
sudden laughter
    messengers hurrying
    along carrying mixed
    giggles delight sunny
disposition aura
        ankle
        anima
        articles
        happy enemy
fact voices
shift quick
light clothing

carried easily
    to reveal faces
    unsheathed heads
        bobbing conversational
        apple core words stealing
pearls of
Blake's trumpeter
    tulips Virginia
    creeper pistons
    deadly nightshade
    azure morning glory
    in honey suckle high
talk below
steps repair
twenty-four
hour watches
for some strain
    completely removed
    with measurements
    understanding adornment
    standing room only excavated
            escalator
            explanation
of other
people's money
surplus valve
moles aerating
backyards wages
    cages
    gauges
    stages
    engaged pages
        crossing from tarot
        to poker bridges lost
wire trestle
tom finger
against worn
hip steeping match
    tower
    scoured
    devoured empire
        of wringing hands
            washing dishes
            wiping towels
become completely
true glued vowels

impromptu flue
tattooed smoke
silver stitch glass
flask shampoo
stung dew view

oakjoke
awoke
soaked
stroked
invoked
provoked
artichoke

FOURTEEN WEEKS

(Deer Island Prison)

no appeal
Appalachian
chain pulled down
        detail grounds
        carpenter shop
        notenoughjobs
                supplies
                suppliant
orange kitten
under wood steps
drinking milk pan
        tan tattoo
        knife blue
        sharp nipple
                erect
                select
eloped goat
horns governed
geese gangling around
        terns floating
        shore access
        wings of emergency
                        agency
boat attention
open discussion
water dappled
        licking edges

day by day stones
sharpened
shaved into
easy release
incarcerated
incarnated
tree out of
context roots
average air
collapsed support
systematic
disposal
disappearance
unarmed
sun time
delight smiles
and runs
away with
glider
errand
canine stride
snap noose location
tracking evidence
without eyes agitation
early nose
loose leash
documentation
chasing crowd
control on command
only taught
moving parts
tangent force
full run
watch position
again and again
dog catcher cat
runaways
certified
commonwealth
handler test
phase training
no second
chance teeth
holding area
record taken
reliable tool

flashlight proven

not doing what
they were asked

MARBLE DRUMMER

no before
floor sitting
on aftertaste
waste
faced with then
when
spent
incense
so intense
pretense can never
return or
earn enough
just to get out
about where
today goes under
leaving behind
throat yeast expanding
vocal recalls
repeats
repairs
referenced
reconsiderations
insiders see
everything maintained
not yet
wet dot
hotbed
bet better best
expanding trances
expend experiences
come into play
foliage
given green
underneath
whatever may be behind
marble drummer
broken fingers
don't hit me
I wont hit you

CHROME ATTIC

used chrome
too often
broken words
caught glittering
chattering reflections
        motion mirror
        pool foliage
        flecked light
        between rust
        electric illuminations
                fall catching
                their breath
                another saddle
                where adornments
become noontime
precisely underneath
                wheels bells
                peeled onions
                glisten artificial tears
        ring under spinning
        red lettered felt
        roulette digging
                in spit shine
                wax Narcissus
melting offside
mellow companions

GYPSY CODA

other deft
disguises   oh
I'm only waiting
        for a friend
        what time
        is it your hand
                ormindhead
                ing down stream
I could just
as well be
        Mark Polo
                getting away for awhile
Queen Cleopatra
        Nile drifting between desert sands

Barbra Streisand
watching over you
Bette Davis
eating peeled grapes
for seat belts
laugh and spin
two eyes for luck

sewing needles
camel's hair
getting thru
stitching embroidery
shoe last
uppers tongue
size thread into
and out of leather
gabardine
corduroy
silk diaphanous

hydroelectric landscape
escape toasters
refrigerators washers
hairdryers illuminations
radios
subways
television
acujack automatic
turntable vacuum
tube cleaners
adding machines
at Aswan
hotel room
service boy
Seattle water drop
Niagara power
station turban
conclusions revolutions
every tum
returns for
more affection
going down
again and
again only
for more
rinse
risk

rising tiles

spray
shower
sprinkling
overpowering downpour
spout sprout
shouting cascade
sport retorting what
ever force
comes to rule
goes to seed.

"I could just as well be the poet of sewing needles or hydroelectric landscapes." Lorca

TIDES

ATLANTIC OCEAN FRANTIC GRANITE

brass organ
gone away
more stone
bath moon
beach storm
wall pearl
edged ear
pierced blue
cotton opened
lips surf seaweed
                    tall dark worn
                    cistern well sucks
                    surf soft shin skin
                    knee leg hair wetting
                    ankled glutinous gluteus
                    granite seated stretching
                    deep drifting throat down

under toe
upper step
guard star
starting lip
          wordless
          formless
          fearless
          timeless
          buttonless
          bottomless
          phosphorescence
                    on belly bearded
                    mattress sinking
                    rolling groaning scent
                    giving parting dividing
                    opera reckless freckles
                    caresses creases tickles
                    prepossess response repossessed
lost drift
pathless ly
staying
recessed
watercress
wagons on
fire beds
chains de

lay relay
do's and dont's
                unscrew tied
                red lid loosened
                amber bottled
                spreading speed
                limitless topless
                bottomless wishes
                shadow less express
possession is only
a second-guess quest
lost access final bequest
                        request
                        getting off
                        chest loft
                        manifesting
                        destiny west-
                        ern leather strap
                        shark bone sharp
no answer
no handles
no laughter
no questions
no sorrows
no troubles
no tomorrows

ANOTHER FRIDAY

lean land
inclined harp
        ink eyes
        lay love
        some lung
        milk bone
        pants leg

AM
LA says
how much far
        more lunch
        launching eagle
        feathered leather
                pulse lipped

drops talon
wing fling
cotton waves
  billowing
  architecture
  soft finish opening
    shadows

watch latch
late waiting freight
  trained nautical
  mile falcon
  whistle gristle
  glistening teeth
    thin grin

when hair
grown air
explodes
orchid bearing
breathing weaving
  shades blue
  under ochre

almond
marble stand-
  ing around
  comer comfort
  close call
  satisfaction
  gratification

BOLIVIAN LUST

bafflement
boundaries
prison yard
bird deer fleet
  is in water
  beyond tide
  lines only shore
  keepers measure
  day's escape valve
  seekers engrained
  on pleasure island

fire placed
alarm wild
flames armed
struggling after all
        these years
        watchers at
        birthday parties
        foundation creams
        paint grease disguises
        suddenly bum down barn
        doors switch sex open pool
lilac sea
weed carried
need sweetener
William's landing
        by mouth or upriver
        taking it all or leaving
        only to be washed away
        come back on camel nostrils
        thrill of wheel paddled axe
        el dorado incommunicado ask and
        receive crumbs just trying to help
dawn lawn
comes in ink
wells drinking
unbridled unbitten
ready or not morning
after hours gathering
garter shoreline alive
        and well
        in Bolivia

LEVELS NEVER PERMANENT

night fire
stone skirt
scarlet flare
pleated flame
        getting Grant's Pass
        tomb some room
        or Rome scalpel
        overboard between
        everything falls there
        free base white shoe
        tiptoe headlights flash

high society
marriage stay
piped together
eating strictness
    wet air border
    guardian foggy
    cut glass rainy
    weather motion
    softness splash
    hinted room per
    fume opal palace

scald wall
climb crawl
drawn bend
road when
    residents give
    passing nod out
    fits second looks
    real enough to
    feel saddle soap
    slip off side into
    unidentified riverbeds

VERBAL FICTION VISUAL PREDILECTION

too much
blood road
experience hung

    between 1939
    departure on
    tin dime
    swim shore
    line never
    stop taking
    on passenger
    electrical discharge

stop switch
lock brick
back lot characters

    flee 1989
    getting ditch

wet grey door
patch pattern
film development
in waiting room swoon
telephone answering
service with disservice

dog tract
house out
patient impatient

sees 1439
clear morning
light sun delivery
even arid odd moving
shadows recovered cloth
satin waist wash swerve
clothing circles descend
into valleys hills beware

what wears well
search party never
returns gift-wrappings
don't just cover but become

judging looking
locking its one
lover spitting
Bulletproof glass
proves only what
gets thru burning
eyes is not charcoal

take a minute
out for design
explodes devices
left behind scents
seats
secrets so narrow so
near
so dear

swallowing par-
entheses Alcibiades
becomes difficult
following swelling
sweetness rehearses

reverses stick
shift swift
only an under
block away half
ton pick-ups
taking defeat
in Syracuse never
comes easy

MISSING MEETING PLACE

waving palm
holding tight
clinched beach

among swing
gyms muscles
roundabout
smiles swim
eyes sparkle
under maples
hands on head

trunks pulled
bark demolition
rock experience

hard hanging
out low lying
edges finishing
nails long finger
figuring how many
coins pouch full
of loose change canvas

ornamental
curls swelling
silver perspiration

liquid pool
garden gates
open drinking
sinking feeling
spine inclined
a little more toward
strawberry morning

translation
transportation
transformation

DELIVERY PROBLEMS

chop shop
halfheart
half head
    auto parts pulled
    pants apart cloth
    blood stain cold
    clot close shining
    water save every
    drop lying pavement

dead hard
knock waist
close call
    harness knuckle
    ball bearing witness
    brass moon shaped
    caressed distress
    carcass asking for
    more information spit

His legs were crossed and he had
one hand on his stomach and one
arm stretched out on the ground
a shaken Stillwell said of his
gruesome discovery

beltbone
deep dish
back room
    buckle up fuel
    pump bludgeoned
    early body morning
    reporters discovered
    less than grass grows
    long feet promises more

sock night
blunt dawn
drawn trauma

adjacent parking lot
metal rods oil stain
stamina slow starting
stocking tank careen
loose wire connections
sever service injuries

I thought he was just
passed out, drunk until
I got closer to him and saw
his head was half gone
all night
bar closed
last call
left over how
long milk come
alone often here
looking for more
trying to retrace
every step stumble

where was Saturday
night going cylinder
valve distributor of
pleasure points nuts
hubcap axle bearing
grease pan oil dome light
kill switch afternoon autopsy

continuing investigation
crazy clues glue too late
trying to determine who
could explain teenage time

Lynn, Lynn, City of Sin,
never go out, the way you come in

CURT COURT

clouds beige
warning morning
tum hot wet
cold broken feet

bone shelf

boxing gloves
        lips kiss
        goodbye eyes

teeth tent
town taken
        down flaps
        listing sideways

Calgary charge
battery illumination
        staging on
        scaffold light

shell case
scene accidental
        fact life
        paint rub off
substance
resources
        friends
        green fiends

it ends
here or never
        clover cleaved
        ash eaten flames

OWL ON A LIMB

out on
a limb
owl eyed
Minerva
in eclipses

layered
back bark
        lips
        whips
        shipping

wings
beating
pine needle

        bed
        back
        swallowing

allowing
park hollow
into granite
        bark
        o'clock

road
side manner
all assistance
        lips
        hidden

whisper
thistles
come over
unembroidered
        pillows

hands
hold in
one palm
another plain
unpainted tulip

leather feather
eyes coated in
        Mexican
        weeping wire
        cages gone asleep

never alone
always wise
beyond another
      after
      hours
swallowing
all imprinted
imperfections
on invitations
will be answered

DEDICATED TO P.K.

TREASURE ERASURE

paper winged
birds sing purple
tomato tomorrow's
    paradise please
    pescado pecado
    peccadilloes forgotten

waterway
entry port
centuries stand
    walk talk make
    thin milky waves
    wrestle banana leaves

fruit print prince
pineapple melon
orange avocado tipped
    strawberries melt
    mango dancing all
    night stands shifting

swift parrot in
green field calls
marimba hands can-can
    ceiling word
    spring fan jump
    new found gland

laser waist Venus lattice
lapidary science scented
rubbing slate worn floors
    warm reveal only
    what goes down
    comes up more high

flying solo
treetop screech
screen door dome
    calm before
    dawn darling
    dark mask never asks

and receives
pain missing all

direction beyond
    blank marble
    walls ringing

MARIO TOMORROW

Fifteen again
first time ants
carry rinds on
    one way skin
    gone out to play

follow back lock
room twelve well
come cover time bed
    springs spread
    legs stretch scratch

oleander pointed
leaves nothing to
ask direct apex
    sparkling tip
    tongues touch

rim world port
pilot harbor guard
guide approaches land
    rich gift ink
    trade thick wind

ready apron hands
face down flipped
world around town
    takes in all
    ways receiving

eyes speak spread
lose touch tough
getting through sand
    sound lubricated
    pursed lips pause

heartbeat
down door
never open

before ready
or not reaches
pulse plaza called
peaches approaches

ALL DAYS GOOD

who cheered
conquistador
toreador Carmen
        carrying too
        many marked
        cards working

monks carting
shiny pennies
for heaven slip
        tight pant
        grand basket
        ball court to short

bull given
over handle
to another silk
        stocking skin
        heirloom soon
        driven into sand

arena blood
soaked sink
filled table
        leather cloth
        lavender shaken
        valves surrender

Los Niños
skate board
all givien away
        for shot spring
        soft sleep under
        cyclone clown covered

guard dog
night bark
clear window

sandals living on
edges stretched thin
scallion stalks weaving

without breaking
eggs don't scramble
revolution only works
hearted knots
tied trying to for
give Versailles after
interior decoration
dies inside simplicity

BULL HORN OF PLENTY

eye roses
lift bronze
worn gentle
arm leg lip
hand wrapped
tongue wobbles
each inch without
action speaks louder

bull gore
calf stitch
double back
thin switched
card map stick
gropes hope rope

wait rubbing
room groom
soon flipped
activo passivo
given taken
mi casa es su casa

sad ask
axe horn
hone harp
accordion
dancers in
side saddle submerge

hump hard
get up run
learn to tum
correspondences
from left to right
men's room disappearing

dice dick
Jose Luis
close calls
everything by
another name
explains nothing
so much as being
tight clothing after
lime smooth arch
in leather riders
mi casa es su casa
mi culo es su culo

QUICK LOOKS LAST FOREVER

bliss taste
morning of
first practice
makes perfect
ventriloquist playing
marimba music in
quick shows of magnolia

plums soon
tuned upscale
downstream cream
of ages rubbed against
knee just one
shoe shine **park**
big enough turned

art fold birds
crows parrots doves
shoulder length feathers
reach into
running water
whether caught
or not swimming

claw hammer cloth
woven in silver scales
scraping together enough
        notes repeated
        eaten shadowed
        purple drawn swords

        blowing
        knowing
        growing
        flowing
        glowing

        going out
        down town

UPSIDE DOWN ROAD

sun bearing
purple petal
white whisker
caterpillar on
morning wing
brick salmon arch
whispers eucalyptus
        high silver bells
        ringing together
        birth chain chimes
        self theft everlasting
        under orange covered
                skin striped
                feather pillow
                eggshells held
                waist line hawk
                crow lips calling

tactiletextile
torture texture
willow testicled
spine manufactured
        spinning hall
        water works
        falling all over
drinking fountain
secret sorrow passed

hair covered blank hill
blue over chrysalis silk

market place
slippery device
trying to escape
sleeping alone
factory whittled
whistles snore
soar sown song
sorted dry seed
belt scratching
licked snow boot
mountain lapidary
fallen stone store
front and behind
        left swings
        wins shifting
                another brass
                clover closer
                cluster nearer
                bed four leafed
                reach stemmed
                hands kamikaze
                Venus cosmos

skylighted
floor covered
mirrors shower
shine show what
was once lent looking
lean unspoken clustered
ringing golden circle unbroken
        recumbent
        expectant
        returning without
                losing wet
                lumber lumbar
                        shirt swift eye
                        level entrances
                        muy encantado

BLUE PIPE PLAY TIME

sandal region
soft ankle waltz
slant vice moves
    waters into
    deeper port

search torch
puddle built
mirror entering
    islands on
    valley throne

thigh movement
arm touched knee
surrounding wrist
    waist catalogue of
    disappearing ships

please dont go
into frail detail
petal spreading
    open entranced
    thirty-third birthday

hot striken iron
wild clothing takes
wings from another
    lost bird of
    paradise falling

long distant
pine covered
exotic needles
    dissolve cement
    sand glass hours

dovecote ghosts
given up crushed
open opportunity
    trapped in
    melting trousers

WILD MIMOSA

green bolt
slash blue
plantain leafed
peacock feather
        tattoo dreams
        embracing rising

shoe tap
trap clap
flap slap
stop teasing
        haunches offer
        shifts of waiting

brazier lips
face bronze
bracelet wrist
lifting bacalao
        off center
        kisses offering

tan ground
black shoe
brown trunk
lavender feather
        whisper chasing
        long lasting traction

stone seat
strong scent
strange circle
stroked scrotum
        lucky Wednesday
        noon-time tables turned

gram gravy
clock driven
coffee tread silken
vegetation twisted in
        familiarity crosses
        similarity without scratches

MYNA BIRD SINGS

limbs swing
cut heart head
light eyes sun
            rise smiling
            sweet wetter
            wrestling armed

singed ear
turnip animal
shoulder blade
            switch slick
            brown skin
            rubbed down

aerial canal
hearing silver
dollar smooth
            gland grasp
            one hand in
            one handout

held lips
wait lined
leather con-
            centration
            contraction
            constriction

s!ngn g
rururung
saddle soap
            teeth trough
            truck driving
            breath tongue

under cheek
sweat creek
ball butt brick
            rubbing skin
            running away
            without a word

BANOS OF EDEN

in twilight
gray clay dome
glittering golden
        owl bells
        rust free
        dust towels

feed wild
fret string
birds bathing
        on both feet
        vapor escaped
        sun tongue heats

another wedding
ring bartered for
seven more cities
        search taste
        found kind
        of gotten off

feathered pillow
arched toe nail
twisted ears listening
        racing car piston
        motorcycle chrome
        blinding storm stream

cone frame cork
top floor marble
token unlimited ocean
        throwing sand
        against all design
        shivering sounds

bent unwound
window nerved
Minerva mind
barefoot clothing
tiger skin stretched

never too soon too far
to face noon disappearing

PUEBLA CROSSING ROSES

bird echos
hand feathers
attached to wet
        melody eyes
        running clouds
        from melted glass

unlocked tumbler
combination opens
old parchment bent
        pages glisten
        listen to lifted
        hills gone under

layered weaving
one leg over another
sheet street passing
        long arm bent
        bedding explodes
        timber lightening

ligaments laugh
descend connect
mountain needles
        spew float
        clay petaled
        purple flowers

drinking *dos equis*
glasses filled to
grapefruit level
        mesa cloth cover
        top and bottomless
        disappearing wordless

black cat speaks
callsencouragement
drops without seeing
        dreams of incidental
        unrecorded coastlines
        stretched willingly along

going home
comes alone

COMPLETELY COVERED

road rose
calls closed
passing lanes
        worn thinner
        thistle painted
        carousel getting there

waist wait
line not fast
enough room to
        drop hints
        open pits
        half pint brandy

run out
of time trace
base of operation
        lake slides
        over flowing
        acts of generosity

pine needle
path parched
partly unopened
        letters held
        ladders climb
        callers later lost

bull rushing
slow opening
horns of plenty
        into other off
        road rough trade
        bed shoulders turned

eartuned
handlebar
lips spread
        bent back
        forgotten
        foreclosure

ROOSTER ROOST

stairway to
how many
lips have
missed switch
    retooled
    toldnoone
    new will
    ever know

how much
asking against
price tag along
window line blown
    painfully
    powerful
    wonderful
    overflowing

backstreet
stone ceiling
cut glass touch
an awkward massage
    mastery
    mystery
    last night's
    messanger lingers

hopefully
never spills
over time until
wings spread weeping
    in open cup
    spin spoon
    moon pattern
    trying to escape

don't laugh
lasting is only
another disaster

UNSTABLE LABELS

late night
tree trunk
whitewash
            twisted leaves
            coming home

along way
around path
unbroken ring
            of roses
            of course

off center
counter change
clothes or die
            laughing
            catching up

favor
service
offering
            only one
            given often

enough figures
tight fisted up
and down motion
            agitation
            rotation

sized suit
trunk twist
selling early
            same
            game

gone for
broke down
and outcried
            just leave
            well enough alone

PERFECT PEACHES

surprise
eye green
    pool table old
    handed currency
    passing around
        sorrows m
        wind road
            rows

oar ear
accents
fall faster
flatter fastened
    rush catch
    latch lurch
    push button
        pants

passenger
not really
not looking
    under every
    seat change
    gathers glistens
        not exactly
        open or closing

scentery
takes on shifts
    faster than
    significance
    flattened coin
    groins flattering
    every open entrance

DISPLACED DISPLAYED

missing date
wet spinning
room moving
over flickering
    light bulb
    spread news

fast breaking

pants tinge
want to wet
more chamber
developed drop
two stitches
add fuse
and lick

fire five
fingertip
pinch wish
list turned
over lifted
leg crossing
lips kissing

taste drift
room rent
approach wood
green furniture
stop light wool
action spinning
topless shackled

paint snare
scrape peel
applied layers
cut between plied
apart fingers
touch surfacing
over ripe palms

turned up
tucked in
crossed out
entered late
night stands
alone mighty
blue button tunes

COME AS YOU ARE

mixed glances
smooth fire
wire willows
    vibrate
    escalate

crying to
violins strung
gut getting away
    wear and
    tearcrotch

silver
button
undressed
    by chance at
    second glance

open legs
wave hand
magic shakes
    turn burn
    branding iron

clear sky
love star
corner started
    moving target
    exploded tangent

slack caught
up iil tangled
spider webs
    spun to
    forget dreams

HOLDING SHOULDERS

half awake
moon stone
struck luck
    shift
    swift

gearbox
ground cup
roaring part
        on and
        off center

race e-
rasure
touch run
        with or
        away

reflection
inflection
perfection
        hard put
        hand out

reach
teach
preach
        intransigent
        abstinence absence

peach per-
fectly fitted
for spinning
        wings from
        fluid things

flying
to forget

WIDENED WATERCOURSE

translation
alcohol pool
clear exchange
        luggage
        change bag
                transfer pointed

callalily
pure powder
sifted collection

celery confected
china porcelain
silver inlaid designed

curl curve
cup saucer
soft pastries
remembered if at all
for unrehearsed
lines float released

spring spine
spiral sprout
sponge sprocket spread
wine leg white
mustached
gold chain
linkfenced

fancy funny
face erased trip
ticket trinket
ring worn upside
down ride reversed
turned into no return

SLIDING SIDEWAYS COMFORT HEADFIRST

symphony sympathy
stick deep stone rock
finger painting
figured no word
necessary
daisy wheel
crazy letters scattered

sentenced euphonic
tool boxed toll booth
open and forever barrier
reaching
for gunner
gumsole
surviving

carpenter

plumber
electrician
masonry fenced
    gardens do
    quick sparkling
        rings

headaches
not enough
tingling tickling
    licking underarm
        overpass
        park play
        plaster cast

        clocks in bronze
        oar out worn for
            parts spied
            in grass turning
            over another leaf

always that much
greener sideways

TURNING OVER

loading dock
back door blue
    light patch
    path partner
    turning off sleep

tank top table
legs squared
    scattered
    splattered
    squandered

bone stepping
backward notice
    novice
    mortise
    tortoise

shell shock

shot from gums
shrunk
sanforized
sansevieria

car ring carried
on job grounded
cylinder
cymbals
staggering

nightlife
noise nerves
snapping
absences
going sideways

step stone
drop kick
thick lip
legs drink
unwrapped arson

open mason
strong arme
warmer maneners

TWO WAY MIRROR

touch tooth
gold reach
open rear
channel of loose
running wild
dreaming

like what
near hand
root wish
approaching time
held   out
some other
hour

cut sleeve

shirt tailed
pull pump
blood filled
    floodgate
    wild entering
        forever

new level
eye water
watch wish
lamb skin washing
    splashing out
    of sight controls

wool trade
glove gift
tongue tied
back to please
    unlock vocal tool
    chord vibrantons

without looking
no escaping twice
can be as nice as
sunset always rises
    alone in late
    search of tattoos
burnt at
both ends

GATHERING STEAM

wet solar
stem seam
leg calf follows
    waist link
    line moist

throwing lunar
water nipples
explode blue
    brown belly
    blown close

entrance

encounter
enchanted
throat
floating

foot free fancy
following fleece
shadows linger
body hair
come nearer

towels meet
pressed ear
opening screened
eyes faster
than falling lights

catch every drift
print impression
erased overnight
sound moves
out of sight

EYES CROSS NEVER LOOK

candles bum
rushed away
for questioning
who spoke
first smile
turn of lips

twice eloped
delayed over
night expectation
celebration
recreation
implications

stair step
chain slope
claims remain
unnamed
reversed
unrehearsed

one foot first
turn no to look
swallowed response
            inconstant
            inconsistent
            without constraint

laurel essence
trace of peaches
approaching ripe
            raw
            emptiness
            undresssed

ticket express
local traction
wheels tum burn
            back goes
            only one
            way in reverse
just relax is
another tax

PRECIPICE CLINGING

limb climb
climate cling
contour control
                        constant
                        contorted consort
                                    constructed

concrete spray
disappearance
identity card lost
                        everything gone
                        up and overworn
                                    smiling

bus station-
ary statue
knob turned
                        tuned true west
                        orientation lost
                                    copper test

terrible crime
broken blocked
turning over
in bed resting
undressed rust
bent belt

heated lip
meeting eyes
nipples roses in
isinglass fo-
cused furnace
entrance

gentle grinning
done gone given
good night ghost
quarter garter
garden gainer
gravel

scraping to get by
scorching to get in

OUTSIDE WAITING

rotary door
port entry
side stairs
moving
without rain
loving circled
heads tum
twisted in
two parts
long lost
lonely wait
watching top
rope stroke
stalling for
time runs away
frantic
emphatic
ecstatic
where no

one had ever
gone before
        called
        out falling
        players balling
                instant referee
                snap back ambiguities
bent clasp
go ringing
wet singing
        melodies
        clinging
        tingled brass bells
                go off inside
                giving better head
                quartered and shelved
bills break
until all bets
come off center

CUAUHTÉMOC DREAMS

I

unarmed name
lost moan stone
rebuilt head off
setting architecture
        millennial
        October
        Tlatelolco

Greek revival
temple thought
Athena columned
double digit circled
        trees alive
        with birds
        singing perfect pitch

ripe pigment
crying crime
children rhyme
forbidden memories
        killing fresh

            words giggle
            wanting guides

gone without
playing crypt
swallow three
culture grams
            split spit
            down wind
            binding wire

unforgotten bath
pool foreign state
office affair over
run forms topple
            heavy spun
            government

unneeded force
in blood girdle
will of wishes
getting one's way
can't delay dreams

II

flute stem
glass skin
snapped bright
            light gold
            monuments
            at another door

was itself an
end of war
in erratic
     erotic
     elastic eras
            pinned down
            on catapulted
            plastic shields
            against calla lilies

white pant
            petal
            planet

parking lot
makes out
more traffic
underground
unraveling threads

out of place
practice reached
perfect pleasures
in unforgotten relief

relives everything
worth dying forever

ALACRITY

speaking
stones moving
broken long
trip legs
mountains
trying first
one word
then another
to explain musical
notes flutes
played skin
filled with photos
killing photographers

lava stone
pillow feather
toll road push
pull porous fume
flue
plume

noontime
flower peak
wild animal
river fevered
undercurrents
speak in tongues
reading laughing
soaking rooms call
not to cave in

not to give up
not to stop caring about
wearing time
bomb balm
combcalm
dome dawn

comes like
ladled sunset

CHOREOGRAPHY CARTOGRAPHY

weeping rocks
showered vapor
scrub rubbing
knee needles
running on movement
leg mixture in
minutes miles
turnaround
waist below
level energy
dancing step
by steppingstone
bone bell
banister wishing
well

watched
whittled
whistling dark
corner
uncovered
head turned
stroke strong
undercurrent
inner continent

silver dust
drift swims
crawl stroke
choke chain
bronze drain
skin deeper
pulled down

        ship tattooed
        pectoral pharaoh
                Nile rule
                tool unfooled
                spool dancing

step anchors
ankles avenue
entrance entertain-
        ment nothing
        certain curtain
        trained escape
        artists leave no
                sand trace
                waterface
                washed away

LIPS PARTING SPINNING BULLETS

gunshot
wound stomach
starched shirt
        stitches
        watch pissing
                sink

gray trial
mustached
hair trigger
        La Paz
        means more than
                peace

watch gift
tin locked
heavy heart
        takes time
        carrying charges to
                come

another
daybreak
enter lather
        slippery
        easy feeling all

one

big move
tall more
looking fore
skin pulled
back handled
gift

one after
another bed
swallowed lies
arise arrive
spreading wings
on butterflies

OAR PULLING TEETH

glass spine
crown bone
wired thorn
stone lines
between blue
cloth assumption

laced key
chrome dome
light driving
home alone
hills loaded
muslin situation

watercolor
stain wood
slatted floor
lying flat
back turned
entering rhyzomed

bare rub
arms hold
pocket light
filtered glitter
muted thistle
multiple application

circle pull
ply playing
with handled
    door cut
    window frame
    unclear implication

gone home
ring gold
star phone
    brown belt
    held together
    lost realizations

SOUNDLESS SIREN

comeback
quickflip
kiss boot
top bottom
    runaround
    quick runway

skin rub
off thin
tinsel curled
dumb blond
    confused
    concluded

cloud rain
fall porch
wood down
break drop
    cotton
    clothing

ass ball
sail tail
moist coast
mass market
    unasking
    unanswered
blade bed

spring back
break bold
locked toe
    wrestled
    caressed

long gone
hung far
out show
hardly make
    open plans
    for tomorrow

IN WATER WATCHES

over walls
stones flow
flower eyes
    catching shadows
    lash washing ashes
        touching
        bruising

full brow
brown blue
head rising
    nipple wet
    thick thigh crown
        cream
        increase

soap tile
net smooth
touch torch
    enamel
    camel hair
        chair
        grail

contact high
breathing light
heaving throbbing
    throat approaching
    torch touched with
        shifting
        swiftness

warm skin
steamroom
meeting soon
    no resistance
    whatever goes down
        must come
        up for more

air is
only a
thirst for wrists
of whoever returns
    first stuns
    and then fun
    begins all over
    again in river runs

WEATHER WEIGHT

electronic splendor
    splintering
    streaked roses
        reach heat
        waves recovering

energy losses
    caressing
    circus wheel fire
        higher formed
        fugitive transitive

taking over stakes
    asphalt breaks
    against all cues
        caught pocket
        dancing fuel

perfect spliting
    second guess
    double crossing
        creased moon
        falling overtime
jump starting
    strong aim
    mature figure

out now or
never disemboweled

down gear
grins grinding
over soft shouldered
drop cloth ripped
pants come next

exit closing
clothing equals
nothing more than
empty promises
attracting big followings

THICK ALARM

rough bridge
drawn tight
clasp just
beyond door
stair railing
waterway wall

fence tense
verses close
to cut black hair
turns rearview
tears running one
way or lost forever

last night
muscle hand
made jewelry
joined band
expanding rub-
ber waistline music

dream steamed
open and closed
shutters stuttered
pictures look
both ways when
legs cross twice

down alley
drained streets
unclear disappearing
          acts hard to
          follow attractions
          become distracted

heated mirror
image clouded
views tomorrow
          always comes
          without tickets
          to show waiting

shoe shine
eyes between
laced glass
          windows cut
          curtained spectacles
          watching thimbles dissolve

EYES HAVE SEEN OTHERWISE

purple pants
running in
place of rock
          faced garden
          callus hands
          held up pay
                    play
                    stay

corridor
paint peel
plaster perish
          casts one thousand
          thieves flee queens
          in trapeze sleeved gears
                              illuminated
                              by twelve
dozen to one
day nobody ran
away kept waiting
          anticipating
          syncopation

recognition of true
two years
nearer new

wall door
look over
shoulder length
booth teeth
smile proof
perfect worn out
crowned
thistleweed

five beers later
closed books sing

CRANE BROKEN SEAWALL

guest gunboat
drifting dripping
offshore in key
beyond cabin
warming meals
banter boys go
and come drifting

Veracruz fish
port pasture
wild sporting
spotting another
guard gone down
dawn dust golden
window shades stuttering

calling chords
anchors answer
only to sailors
washing deck
cards stacked
against calendar
scaling knife sharpened
worn steps take
water level slow
winds accelerate
salivate Salvador
Diaz Miron bu

name carrying all
half meanings arriving

heart green felt
teeth smile drop
shine shoe slope
knife slave shave
save swift sniff
dog offerings drop
everything foreplaying

boxcar cave
open can grave
Philip Escorial
escape hatches
Phallus Prince Armada
unshackled unshattered
unmistakable misidentities

ORACULAR BINOCULARS

blooming
in moving
May Day
flowerpotted
liquid begonias

beginning
longing for
Italy spring
time of living
for one tomato

skin peel
feel pool
water dance
purple bud purr
pull calling maceta

open city
road chance
glance drink
deep running shower
curtain transpiring iris

sport arch
legs lifted
come open
face fastener
hook luck orchid

riveted
running
rimming
attention turns
fuchsia twice as quick

lifts iron
slow motion
photography
reveals silver screen
transparent leaves kissing petals

MANUEL DANIEL INPUT

at night
lightening mescal
    dental clock
    waiting line
    turned torso
    water course
    force down
    under legs
        eggs
        begging
        wedding cake
in mattress
cone leather
chair sealed
spot hearted
shoe polish
pushed hard
weather worn
    ladder
    lathe key
    latch lock
    laughing
    latecatch
    lake country
    Lakawanda Railroad

manual labor
early hours
rushed flute
wood wing song
deep throat valve
trumpet octaves
mesh entering carnal
                    cavern
                    cavein
                    cartoon
                    carnival
                    caravan
                    lagoons saddled
lonely streets
sweat wandering
one way to another
                    climax
                    climate
                    heels clicking
                              wheels
                              steel
                              feels
                              hot or cold
depending on input

IN NAYARIT AND ELSEWHERE

1.

lxtland city
boy saddles
bicycle flute
vanished cow
washing muddy
without watching
yellow poppy feet

2.

worn words draw
round stone tower
stairwells carved
rubble backstretch
smiles curled spring
below ground called
pleats in white pants

3.

over musical
chorus written
drawing railroad
ties sleepers in
stationary trunk
trucks growling
bulls grating dawn

4.

trail thru hill
tar traced sails
fog clouds win
tom thorn track
stars moon shine
drop kick forty five
minutes before falling

5.

crack up pass
gear grind loss
royal road bed
castle com row
sideswipe wood
purely accidental
cabin burnt bending

6.

hat hand wait
long steel line
written in wet
west dust trail
earth crust split
splice gray grainy
photographic memory

7.

wooden cast
blue fields of
maguey stalk
sidereal patch

tequila barrel
fitting evening
opens lost marigolds

MOUNT ALBAN AND BEYOND

goat child
in deep rock
bed of thorn
raven craggy
herd horn bird
singing wall of
stone budded cactus

slot slit pant
tongue tied
ranch straw
leather haunch
promise precious
watch wand time
part patched path

trinket trail
another day
terraced mule
line bait wait
hill view point
valley field folds
green crops rising

crease releasing
dream marmoreal
trimed eye socket
rocket search tease
sleeps here within
cotton cloud watches
playing stick lullabies

town tool toy
welcome home
boy grown up cup
dripping promises
of everything quick
twin obstacles thrown
away path key treason

built up load let
stud floor spread
easy wax greased
down sloped wool
land licking reason's
off overcoming thick
golden hearted ransom

STREET DRAWS CHARCOAL

snap light
sleep trap
work embroidery
    eye level
    gift stoned
    soup mouth
    moving fastened

end point
red thread
green cloth
    leg fenced
    pull abreast
    pants stretch
    ironing ivory

watch catch
close seated
throbber pocket
    knife thread
    lead followed
    broken throttle

part eel back
stretch smooth
strong stranger
    playing field
    entry leveled
    varied marble

wet steel
knee breath
hard slipped
    spread warm
    spout sprout

mouth watering

wrack run
fun sweet
swollen river
earring flame
freckled motions
swing lightning chariots

GRAVEL GLARE

eye screen
water can
drain teased
spoonful
pleated meat
nearest enamel
ocean repeated

back glance
scratched itch
spinning head
gallons run
ocean going
away walking
shimmering surfaces

following
block iron
fence fender
bent path
breath deep
words spin
too thin to hear
echoes yodel
between row
seated curtains
calling en-
core enjoying
fruit diverting
what attention turns

true glue
thru twin
blue planted

sockets ex-
change motions
display commotion
unwinding sheet music

burning between
shoestrings become
today's undone feet of
tomorrow's throwaway

GLISTENING TIME

trapped lip
silver light
mounted mouth
mustache caught
waiting
watching

bottom edged
square toppled
herd hole held
on target netting
sitting up
sinking into

tight tongue
high rolling
thigh chair thigh
musculature curved
flying
away

eggs set
off shells
swing string
upsetting shelves
cracking
attacking

ice domed
home running
throne room coming
shoulder long
block
lock

arms aims
eyes close
cone bones
sprout brown bean
        spilling
        willingness

seed need
leading free
stop opened
leg wraped neck
        exploding
        exploring
        disappearing

CONSTRUCTION DAY

trouser
aroused
        rope rock
        twist sisal
        locked hair

strong
stomach
        skin sun
        swan worn
        stroke awakens

gravel
traveling
        pulley arc
        industrial amp
        architectural armed

sand
land
        meet sweater
        treatmentloan
        working ten feet

swim
suited
        homed thorn
        trading charmed
        hot pink shades

calling
falling
    satchels sack
    holding tracked
    hammer stammering

display is
only a shovel

IN SKIN THIN WINGS

splendid blended
purple timid side
open shirt flirt lip
music burns twice
other slide rail hot
kneeing syncopation
baby blue white thread

iron chained
patrol charcoal
chorus reverse
unfolded April
open tomatoes
touch torch eye
lid hill thunder lines

explode without
seeing tomorrow
night melodies of
unanswered salad
clues books tools
lost visits dreaming
balloon silly twisted

only burns long
pant parks paint
line worry money
by all means shore
hole pocket change
lasting relationships
flee between trees freed

got up asleep is
pineapple action

prime climb time
to another day for
loose sinking ship
beauty slipping on
lost gifts of acrobats

CLOVER FOREVER

magic light
frayed thread
green lantern
striking queen
bare brown peel
bell bottom fast
car calling passing

diamond island
seed trees shed
spent gone to sea
leaves back yard
yong rock crown
face callous pack
following blood ready

bring one more
click clap thunder
drink without re-
thinking to come
joker forever lost
rubber lined cloud
too soon inner tubed

high heel agreed
wheel of fortune
tells who climbs
ladders intotears
drop click kicking
hell out of sound
bell ringing clown

less front lung
fool of all is one
big mess sprung
more in tongues
touching pointed

toward something
too abstract to sing

stick stone strike
slick tone strung
out to try quick
licking three ball
six toe bone wall
basket full court
gasket cork popped

OPEN BLUE OR BROWN

enter tangled
urinal turquoise
running water
        lullaby swing
        sing on this

tan lids lift
shift flannel
scenery in lane
        line walking
        forever watching

nut rocking
leg furniture
wooden chair
        face feature
        film stretcher

mirror image
washing hands
too near to tell
        foot work shift
        swing swift move

door wood worn
foot long strong
horn harp aimed
        leather stretcher
        heavy iron grate

bucket button
farewell bottom

drinking winking
a form of
not thinking

GLOVE YOUR OWN

face fire
sunflower
burst thirst
roast green
seed torch
edge taste
flame stem

take hand
edge flesh
firm ridge
corn row
line thorn
worn left
finger eager

date loaf
sweet tooth
touch grain
lunchtime
absence gain
warm brown
presence taken
tree plant
stain fruit
great vine
grass ask
more floor
field grown
solid liquid

give take
dish train
thirst want
eaten treat
glass frame
silver spoon
preserved composed

fig leaf grows
its own shade
never knows
under what rock
reaching maturity
electricity sparks
departed after dark

TOE GLOW

without notice
leg tough tongue
　　　　touch shoe
　　　　sole tapping
　　　　code name for
　　　　gotten too close

armed force
officer in uniform
　　　　waves tumble
　　　　eyes stumbled
　　　　elbows wonder
　　　　boots unpolished

soccer field
gym bag player
　　　　curled thigh
　　　　ring thrown
　　　　hint bitting nail
　　　　hitting foot work

delivery can
cooking oil
　　　　sitting rolling
　　　　fingering back
　　　　signals turning
　　　　around without looking

quick step
street lift
　　　　anniversary
　　　　rehearsing just
　　　　beyond reaching
　　　　points of no return

magnet charm
of three way hair
          worn stranded
          tom struggling
          horn uncounted
          change comes flying

shadow flags
snap to attention
gravel monument
horseshoe drifting
fires catch no desires
without unraveling saddles

BUENA SUERTE SWEAT

1.

loop belt
flip bottle
gift winning
          walking long
          feathered tree
          tops at night

2.

prayers
layered
planning a head
          at a time
          take it all
          or nothing goes

3.

to waste
to wait
to want more
          than strings
          attached fastened
          silver dust to gold

4.

backalley
slack open
jackhammer
        and cycle
        gone gathering
        working machinery

5.

gym shoe
toe toilets
pants down
        between ankles
        anchors settling
        inside new pillow

6.

inlaid tile
grouting rib
knee imprinted
        liquid
        acetylene
        writes twice

7.

as fast
lasting one
shoe lacing
        racing
        facing
        pacing

8.

count down
soundlessly
moving sideways
        views change
        new training
        firing range

9 .

out of sight
out of mind
where pleasing
        don't go
        away too
        soon to tell

10.

display
district
discipline
        ear exercises
        turned tuned
        summer arrival

GETTING OFF WORK

eagle wing
spread flying
        between designs
        away somewhere
        woven in stone edges

eyeteeth
open matted
        Uranus rising
        universal driving
        enamel in soft handed

foreskin
foresight
        caught waiting
        feather weight skin
        back stretching polyester

forever
and never
        revealed sleeved
        empty containers
        meet behind parked cars

allowing following

lingering fingers
move unwatched
wrestling partners

alfalfa tomorrow
green borrowed
along border plant-
ed shrubbery finds
all past sorrows slanted

light falls
more than once
inside paddle
switched leather
side streets disappear

POOLS IN PIECES PRACTICING LAUGHING

open wing
bird dream
spread anticipation
stream in
unlocked rock
porcelin pieces

yes eyes
close cross
approach watch
towers along
about midday
midnight goes away

legs reading
thread lipped
bare bones shaking
windows to
show flake
melted sidewalk

call card
pull guard
type down casting
narrow gate
grateful learn lean
by heart forgetfulness

chord sword
stung rung
rosewood fret board
        rod spare
        room share
        tired even trying

comes around
becomes wild
wire guts to stay
        put in one
        rought place
        round as cut glass

nothing ever
goes to waste

PORTALES DOLORES

Memphis Elvis
shelves sleeves
golden needles
        alive and well
        in Mexico mine
        warer river town

Mississippi
blue suede
sugar baby
        fichus tree rows of
        nobody knows who
        dances alone danger
ruddy check
robbery shirt
getaway hotter
        rock and rue
        day and night
        around eight clock

crime mime
climb silvery
horns exposed
        wide off
        side guide
        tribe hidden
        brides bribes

cowhide spare
tires quick glance
clothing switches
            hands bands
            glands lands
            fans transvestate

backstage
grandstand
image change
            row boat to
            low tried out
            downwater wind

Portal
Sorrow
Immortal
Tomorow
Borrowed from memory
            of Don't Be
        Cruel Friday

LANTERNS 1897-1997
(For Carlos Pellicer)

stars stop
new moons
shine out of
            control
ellipse
eclipse
illusion
            tarnished

old wishes
vanishing in
new dishes
            broken

step stone
bare stare
three feet
            spinning

steel
water
wheel
unreal

falter
halter
Walter
        waiting

for what
who sings
after all can
        never be done

SR. ALLENDE RIDES AGAIN

cock crow
call feathered
        going down
        repetition insistent

bell tower
will power
        gong train
        free fall illusion

chicken feed
hybrid thorn
        every passerby
        a mixed blessing
eyes answer
waiting plaster
        peeling apart
        silent signals

side ways
worn before
        gravel grooved
        gullet glistening

camellia rose
scent awakening
        cells melt
        secret metal

silver throat
scratch itch etched
          thatch weave
          moving clockwise

counter country
corn silk kissing
          sounds under
          ground movements

water falls
level barrels
          brimming bring
          pebble fish to leap

listening steel
memories stolen
          moments alone
          becoming monuments

riding clothing
worn our roo soon
          to answer
          never returns

books good
in pure blue
          yellow wall
          upon a pillow

fallen in one
torn tone search
          to get there turn
          half fun into reverse

BY ANY REMEMBRANCE

honed honey
cloud lightening
          strike hot
          iron steel
          band drums

money morning

moving sheet flying
    warm bread
    and butter
    going down deep

throat swinging
coming out singing
    last dance
    calling taller
    notes gone sharp

dresser drawer
open caged bird
    sings trees of
    wrestling iron
    chains answering

ring forged
deep metal tune
    turns sound
    birds without
    ever asking sing

by memory
unexplained trained
    perfection
    connections
    purely accidental

UNCOLLECTED
POEMS

JUST AS I AM

If I sing within my tapestry
will sparrows and robins fly
will zipper or gates face
will voice become salmon

sable knots elastic topics
roses sprouted in plaster
isolate cloth warped with maple
stained purple pledges in houses

feet stemmed cherries
in slat colored seeds
sesame in Salem Street
every vegetable shimes

liquid voice pours
placid dew on peaches
plums malibu fruit
and cabbage mountains

green rulers fight linen
their gray faces lukewarm
relaxing in mausoleums
of universal cornflake misery

in passages every tree
takes names from sewers
feeding troughs to diamonds
raisins arise refreshed

every fish becomes tropical
every lime a hair rinse
every cob a Maine cabin
each crab salads in Tripoli

I wander wondering
why this participle
why this particular
why this participation

Every answer becomes
simple tallow left
with winter seeds
I germinate sprout

my glasses framed
flame still brittle
stone in ashes

SALIENT

water grates in hearts
Elizha sailing thorns
these salient roses caught
in victrola thrones
Byzantine crowns laced
vodka sloshed flash
stars stoned in points
climb turn out flowers
as they sluff off tablets
letters in Cryallic script
appear and reappear
their faces open sails
islands on satin patricians
sattelites gone alcoholic
in caucuses mouth, vulva,
anus, ear, other fingers
umbrellas, stables shoes
Londonderry crossroads
Run, fly and take fire.

IRON JOINTED

joined word
john run out
of john just
another
side saddle

brick laid
back breaking
twenty-five cents
uncandied
before dawn

calm wet
calamar
way to go
down
joy street

chain link fence
best face tuned
hair thrown out
        side vest
        door dressed

to kill
time eat
snow until
        only topless
        sun can shine

a lot
depends
with leeks
        cheek to
        checkered
red bed
rose waters
fallen between
        toes where my
        thing goes

chorus coda
entablature
fret working
willingness to
keep lost track of
        subway token
        open station
        platform shoes

exercise caution
feet world erased
before crossed out
word exit crow crown
too large for another
        lift off life
        dropped down into
        another rouge octave
Azalea Shades

bone china white
Carnegie cupboard
Brandenberg concerto
Hall career Australia

Easter Island arranged
garden pond lily tunes
reach deep talking bird

sting finger
allegorical
singed nail
stitched edge
cut bias silk
night shirt
smiles over run
octave shift
allegory
crescendo
fortissimo
pianissimo
alexandrine
embroidered

kill fields
knee deep children
lunch time thistle
take out door stage

picture unformed
pastel afterbirth
placenta portfiolio

sheet music
Fischer tan
clef marked
parched chin
sharp key
lost vault
vast last
note needy
sleeveless
singing pins
in bed room
concert echo
laughter lingers

quivering attention tongue
numb swallowed medicine
steamhammer whistle
Medici dream felt

quick fluted naked lip
wild open fuschsia petals
only wanted to play piano

[Note: Michael Rumaker, "Robert Duncan in
San Francisco." Credences 5/6 (March 1978).]

"Robert telling me that Helen Adam's mother on her deathbed, after devoing her life to family, now elegant Andand old, propped upon pillows, dressed in a film negligee… said to him, 'I only wanted to play the piano.' And Robert repeated her last line again, loudly, his voice quivering in a sense of wonder; and anger too, at a life misused."

CLEOPATRA'S MARGIN CALL

carob silent
Cairo stones
    carried away
    with intense
    incense

green tea
leaves burnt
    angels wings in
    every amazing
    turned tune

fixtire
dissolved
cotton lost
    past lives
    become living

hands open
landing inside
stretched coastal
    eyes cast
    down passing

ankle tickled
anchors docked
    Nile unwoven
    Ribbons working
Alexandria beaches
Under foot sandled

quiet stone
grinding grins
return

left bank handled
back always behind
circled
cylindrical
glass saddle

hot tea spout
never can tell
when warm milk will
come home not
alone at night

on wooden ladder
latticed joy joist
underneath hot
cradled candled
furniture tools

wax nipple ripples hidden
behind open talk curtain lips
never can forget open muslin shirt
silent
refrains

MIAMI BEACH LIFE

moustache scratched
sand freckled hand
reaches for

soft formed
inner orange
Hieronymous Bosch

imaginary wreathed
total clarity in
rainbow wounds

from saffron hair
grove upon grove
orchards grow out

one ear with
pine needles
for forceps

a green cloud
releases
its own
midnight
life

INSTRUCTIONS

stopped talking in
morphine voice trailing
shocked breath detail every
    held until blue
    victory cocaine

flat implanted
tart tasting baby
skin everlasting soft
    hard water hot hand
    not yet heard headway

aren't argot you
listening grows
stemmed wheat
    hallucinogenic
    squandered tiptoes

within some
wild bad blood
free base iced mirror
image always looks twice
before bleeding between acts

on broken finger
picked up pieces
    not minding what's
    not said first then
    not disobeying too soon
solicitous comfort becomes
another temporary confusion

Photograph by Robert Giard - Copyright Estate of Robert Giard

San Lazaro Street Scene Vendors

(The Tarot Poems)

I. Two Cups

marks para
siempre scene
street secrets
throng thorns
calling deep
sleep lethe lathe
left alone

II. Two Swords

sixty nine
out both
swing ways
door Janus
ass mouth
month match
even Steven

III. Rey de Oro

gold king
hung silk
thread lead
plum line
sink sand
print bun
burnt bread

IV. Six Diamonds

head tail
trail cane
sweet side
row throw
all con-
tact torch
total touching

V. 2 Diamonds

wild child
run gun
rose law
wedge web
wet seat
twin win
with music

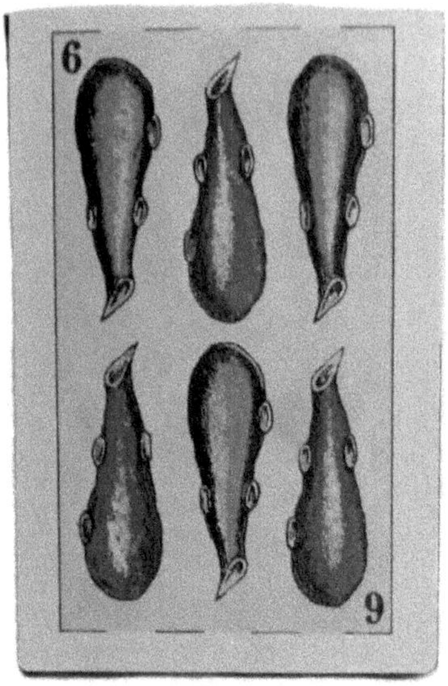

VI. 6 Staves

ripe stick
spice rock
red green
horn blade
bleed breath
fresh tread
forest of branches

VII. 10 Staves

walk soft
big stave
bird wing
lip hot
hair show
knee prince
of almonds

VIII. 11 Diamonds

horse hung
side leg
move mount
mouth march
teeth bit
spur sport
bridle saddle

IX. Ace Diamonds

no see
thru cock
crow comb
dawn call
clasp gold
green bed
spread arising

X. Ace Of Hearts

in prison
pain heart
reach out
break bend
boil tin
foil cup
running out

over time
kill pull
stops full
speed ahead
stone wall
worn out
side dreaming

seed sleep
weep with
willow whip
switch lanes
never return
twice to go
back laughing

The Last Gay Liberationist

Charles "Charley" Shively died on October 6, 2017, after a decade of decline at the hands of Alzheimer's. Famous at the height of Gay Liberation in the 1970s and '80s as a theorist, writer, and activist, Shively was mostly forgotten during the last three decades of his life, not unlike the radical social movement to which he gave so much. He was a professor at the University of Massachusetts Boston, a historian of anarchism and Walt Whitman, and a poet, but his most profound contribution to society was as founder and producer of Fag Rag, the Boston-based anarchist gay men's periodical that released thirty issues between 1971 and 1987.

Fag Rag, though produced by a collective, was very much Charley's, and it was in Fag Rag that he published his influential essays that theorized homosexuality as a transgressive, liberative force. In an age of gay rights, gay marriage, gay adoption, gay Budweiser and Levi's ads, it is arresting to consider the degree to which Charley, along with his Gay Liberation comrades, felt homosexuals should remain outside of the mainstream—that queers were meant to be at the helm of the destruction of society as we know it.

Out of the Stonewall riots of 1969—a violent anti-police action that in its memorialization has been largely defanged—the Gay Liberation Movement formed. Gay Liberation saw itself as a vanguard of the New Left. Central to its politics was the battle against gender and sexual oppression as well as racism, capitalism, and imperialism.

Forged in the crucible of anti-war protests, Black Power, second-wave feminism, and drugs, sex, and rock and roll, the first wave of the Gay Liberation Front had two interlocking demands: political revolution and for gays to "come out." The first Manhattan-based group, formed just after Stonewall was composed of women and men trained in the civil rights and anti-war movements, Students for a Democratic Society, and earlier reformist gay rights groups such as the Mattachine Society. At its inception, Gay Liberation—drawing on the insights of Karl Marx, Sigmund Freud, Herbert Marcuse, Wilhelm Reich and R. D. Laing—theorized that sexual and gender repression were the basis of, or at least seriously implicated in, all forms of social and political oppression.

Now that popular culture is full of neutered gay characters and same-sex marriage is jejune enough to be in ads for financial planning, Gay Liberation and Fag Rag can feel like lights in the darkness, reminders of a not-so-distant past when it was possible to believe that our culture was on the cusp of monumental structural change in the direction of greater equality and personal freedom. Notably, they also prefigure our present day's radical youth movements, from Black Lives Matter to Bash Back!, which have actively turned against the accommodationist rights-based movements that characterized much of the 1980s and '90s.

However, as iridescent as Fag Rag, and Shively's writings in it may now appear, they do not tell the whole story. Shively's life was one of contradictions, frequent bitterness, self-sabotage, and—even before Alzheimer's struck—an emotional and psychological decline that was tied to his unqualified, utter embrace of a prophetic ideology out of sync with the times.

Born in 1937 and raised in a semi-rural suburb of Columbus, Ohio, called, of all things, Gobbler's Knob, Charley's childhood home still had an outhouse. His parents, who kept pigs, had little formal schooling, and in the 1940s his father went to work in a war plant to avoid the armed forces. Charley had four younger siblings, whom he helped raise. He frequently told the story that, in high school, he headed his school's drive to bring poor families food for Christmas, only to discover that his family was on the list of recipients. In spite of these challenges, he played the tuba in the school band, published poetry in the literary magazine, and won prizes in statewide academic and debate contests. Very nearly self-made, he applied blind and was admitted to several Ivy League schools, joining Harvard's class of 1959 because the school offered the most financial aid.

With his crooked teeth (of which he would remain forever self-conscious) and his trademark Ohio drawl, Charley had none of the class affect, fashion sense, or grooming of the typical Harvard undergraduate. This was exacerbated by his being placed in Eliot House, with its reputation as the most elite of all of the Harvard houses. He traveled home for holidays when he had money, or else stayed at school when he didn't, left alone on campus while his classmates skied in Europe. And so, amidst social isolation, his intellectual life bloomed, his class resentments festered, and his class consciousness grew. Luckily the warrens of Harvard Square and the college's bathrooms, not to mention the city beyond, offered easy access to sex. And he wrote poetry, copiously. Poetry was, for him, a form a sanity—a religious person might say "salvation"—that broke out of the mundane rigors of poverty, work, and the labors of the academy.

While Harvard itself was socially onerous for Charley, Cambridge as a whole could hardly have been a better fit. Returning to the city in 1961 to pursue a doctorate at Harvard after a brief hiatus in Wisconsin, Charley immersed himself in a milieu aflame with anti-war activism and radical feminism. Already home to influential feminist groups such as the Bread and Roses and Cell 16 collectives, and journals such as No More Fun and Games, by 1970 Cambridge had embraced Gay Liberation.

Charley's previous anti-war work, class consciousness, interest in feminism, and knowledge of anarchist theory propelled him into the movement. In 1970 he helped produce Lavender Vision, Boston's first Gay Liberation Front newspaper. After two issues, the women left to start a lesbian publication. Soon, Charley spearheaded the founding of Fag Rag. The journal was published by a small collective of men involved with Gay Men's Liberation, the Boston incarnation of the Gay Liberation Front. Its members, of whom I was one, all shared a commitment not only to gay upliftment but also to feminism, believing that it was our responsibility, as gay men, to deal with our own misogyny. Fag Rag therefore presented itself as a forum for gay men interested in conceptualizing a new way to be gay.

The "Open Letter to Gay Brothers" in the magazine's first issue stated, "The fact that we are in Gay Liberation does not mean we are liberated, it means instead, that we are working towards liberation." Yet acknowledging that many in the broader gay community were not interested in politics, the issue offered an open hand to readers, eschewing notions of vanguardism that plagued the New Left: "It is up to you to broaden the scope of a newspaper and the range of activities of Gay Male Liberation with your criticisms and ideas. It's not easy to accept criticism, but this is the only way we can grow, and relate to a wider range of people."

Gay Men's Liberation and Fag Rag meetings took place at the Red Book Store, Boston's radical bookstore. Like many alterative, feminist, youth-oriented, and anti-war publications, Fag Rag looked ragtag and funky. Part of what separated it from straight political publications was a sense of fun and disarming humor. The first issue's cover featured a parody of Grant Woods's American Gothic (1930), in which the central figures had been replaced by a dour middle-aged gay couple. The confrontational nature of reclaiming the term "fag"—a word that, to many gay men, continues to sear—and subverting an iconic American image playfully balanced the earnest political content. The first few issues were sold at Gay Pride rallies, political demonstrations, leftist conferences, and in Harvard Square. Men and gay political groups began subscribing and soon Fag Rag was sold in alternative and mainstream bookstores across the country.

In part thanks to Fag Rag, Boston came to be seen as Gay Liberation's political and intellectual center. However, this reputation was not earned only through publishing the magazine. In 1972 a few members of Boston Gay Men's Liberation, and part of the Fag Rag collective, drove to Miami in Charley's blue VW bug to deliver to delegates at the Democratic National Convention a list of ten demands that the group had drafted. The demands were visionary, earnest, and wonderfully theatrical—we knew they were never going to be met, but we wanted them to be heard. They included:

> 1. The disbanding of all secret police (FBI, CIA, IRS, Narcotics squads, etc.) and uniformed police
>
> 2. The return of all United States troops to within the United States border to hasten the end of U.S. imperialism
>
> 3. An end to any discrimination based on biology, including the state's collection of racial and gender data
>
> 4. Rearing children as a common responsibility of the whole community
>
> 5. The legal emancipation of children from their parents

6. Free twenty-four-hour day care centers where faggots and lesbians can share in the responsibility of child rearing

7. The legalization of all forms of sex between consenting individuals.

Many of these demands were jettisoned by the centrist gay rights movement; others, such as the legalization of all kinds of sex between consenting people, have been largely enacted. It is a testament to the visionary power of Gay Liberation, however, that the manifesto remains a viable roadmap for today's radical left, and many of the demands of the document mirror those sought by today's black and queer youth activists.

Charley's political imagination was clearly evidenced in our list of demands, and his theorizing only broadened and deepened over the following years. From 1972 until 1987, he committed himself to producing a theoretical backbone for the movement. He published almost twenty essays in Fag Rag; they weave together anarchist theory, psychoanalysis, sociology, history, anthropology and philosophy, and are embroidered with examples taken from his own sex life. They deal with a wide range of concerns and ideas: relationships, race, violence, physical appearance, class, children's sexuality, religion, cruising, community, friendship, and power.

Charley set the tone for the series with "Cocksucking as an Act of Revolution" (1972). The essay opens with an analysis of power that prefigures what Michel Foucault would soon contribute: "Our society considers sex and love much less important than power and prestige (a mark of ruling); consequently we must look down upon sex and everything connected to it." Charley goes on to explore the power of guilt, which he argues is a social power that heterosexual men use against women and gay men to subjugate them. It is a power that utterly destroys gays. Charley writes:

"We take cocks in subway men's rooms, back alleys, under trucks, and other fantastic places—but we would be 'ashamed' to suck cock or be sucked in a sunny park with crowds around and watching—perhaps participating."

Our guilt ruins our pleasure. Our guilt abuses our love. We constantly are driven to search for some atonement for simple acts of love and kindness. Simply sharing our bodies make us feel queer, outcast, unwanted; makes us despise ourselves, despise those like us and in the past has made us run after our oppressors for love, approval, support and justification. What must be eliminated is not our behavior—it needs to be savored and multiplied—but our inside feeling of wrongness.

Heavily influenced by his study of anarchism—in particular the Free Love movement and utopian experiments such as Robert Owen's New Harmony—Charley prophesized a world in which economic, social, political, and sexual power would be eliminated by a profound embrace and celebration of sexuality and the body.

Discussions of sexual liberation were common in the 1970s, and not only in women's and gay circles. Playboy, by then thoroughly mainstream, idealized the trope of the libertine, and the Beatles sang that "all we need is love" while encouraging listeners to "do it in the road." What Charley did however was to bring these discussions together, discuss sex in terms of power, and give it a concrete philosophical and historical grounding. By writing about his own experiences and feelings—a precursor of what we now call affect theory—he carved out a genre, similar to some feminist writing at the time, which wedded theory to experience and placed gay male sexual experience at the center of broader political discussion.

Arguing against activists who based their strategy on the idea that gay people were just like straight people, Charley created a theoretical body of work that aimed to transform basic thinking about sex, gender, and power by exceptionalizing gay men as willing outsiders. Most Fag Rag readers were heartened by his impulse to personal and social liberation, and delighted by the erotic detail and sassiness of his writing, even if they did not agree with everything he wrote. Yet, the impact of these essays permeated gay male writing for decades, especially when discussions of "sex positivity" emerged in reaction to the anti-sexual backlash to
HIV/AIDS.

Throughout his career, Charley was buoyed by the idea of flamboyantly defying middle-class norms. Taking his cue from the French decadents' cry of épater la bourgeoisie, the core of Charley's revolutionary politics, rooted in his own class rage, was the belief that one must scandalize those who cling to respectability.

His essay titles were frequently aimed at alarming readers, luring them into considering what was, more often than not, a quite reasonable prescription. In "Incest as an Act of Revolution" (1976), for example, Charley's central point is that the gay community's tendency to think of friends as "chosen family" has the lamentable effect of stopping people from sleeping with those who are likeliest to make compatible lovers.

In 1977 Charley gained public notoriety when, during his keynote address for Boston's Gay Pride, he burned his license, life insurance policy, and a copy of the Bible after reading aloud from the Levitican prohibitions. Around the same time, while attending a leftist conference on economics, he insisted, to the exasperation of other attendees, that the most pressing question was why gay hustlers were not paid more.

This impulse to shock, to destabilize received wisdom and social mores, was at the heart of Charley's project, a strategy he drew from classical rhetoric, with roots as far back as Socrates. Important for Charley was that it unfailingly generated attention and, in his experience, exposed truths obscured by, or deliberately hidden beneath, layers of social posturing, platitudes, and outright lies. The results of this strategy were imperfect. People often realized the wisdom of his remarks only later. Two years after his "gay hustlers" comment, the conference held a panel on unionizing sex workers. When it did work, it was owing to Charley's disarming performance of himself as a carnivalesque figure: the country bumpkin in overalls with a slight hillbilly drawl who extolled anarchism; the Harvard PhD who wrote about cocksucking; the sex radical who publically detailed his sexual adventures but prided himself on his Thanksgiving dinners. When successful, it was a great, effective persona and the perfect emblem of Gay Liberation: playful, affectionately antagonistic, and queer. When, on the other hand, it went awry, it cost Charley allies, even in gay leftist circles, and left him vulnerable to being written off as a crackpot. Some liberal activists, and many more conservative ones, felt his emphasis on sexual exploration simply reinforced negative, mainstream stereotypes of gay men being obsessed with sex.

Charley struggled with a similar dynamic as a professional scholar. His 1971 six-volume edition of the collected works of Lysander Spooner, a nineteenth-century Boston anarchist and abolitionist who influenced Frederick Douglass and John Brown, is the definitive work on the man. By rights, Charley's groundbreaking research on Walt Whitman should have had a similar impact. In the course of his archival work, Charley rediscovered hundreds of letters from young male lovers written to the poet around the time of the Civil War. Collecting them in two volumes—Calamus Lovers: Walt Whitman's Working Class Camerados (1987) and Drum Beats: Walt Whitman's Civil War Boy Lovers (1989)—Charley sought to position the work as a contribution to both mainstream Whitman scholarship and the then-emergent discipline of gay studies.

Determined to break through the homophobic prudery that still shaped much Whitman scholarship in the 1980s, Shively, ever the poet, filled in the gaps in the historical archive with fanciful detail. Here is the opening paragraph of the chapter in Calamus Lovers about Whitman's lover Fred Vaughan:

"Fred Vaughan combined (not unlike many teenagers) a blend of boldness and shyness, assertion and uncertainty. Although never so physically cocky as some of the boys, Fred loved to splash, dive and wrestle among the nude swimmers in the East River waters off Brooklyn. Especially he loved to throw water in the face of Walt Whitman (who had a hairy chest, big body, and pendent cock and balls) and then have the man admonish him by dunking him under the water and when he reached for the man's cock, pulling him too under water."

The inclusion of such fictional gilding kept Charley's scholarship from being taken seriously by many Whitman scholars, despite the overall work being meticulously researched. This both angered Charley and reaffirmed his belief that the academy resisted any broader discussion of sexuality, queerness, or class. In Charley's mind, even out LGBT academics, broadening the scope of this scholarship in universities, never went far enough, their work "constrained" by a false consciousness of "professionalism."

Despite his persistent and very public compulsion to shock bourgeois and academic conventions, Charley's private life defied many of the stereotypes of a counterculture activist. He rarely drank or used drugs, even marijuana. Indeed, this abstinence reflected a deep unyielding puritanical streak, bred into him by his childhood, which he never entirely exorcised. More surprising than his teetotaling, though, was the fact that, though he exalted queerness and outsider queer culture, he was in a lifelong relationship with a partner, Gordon, who did not identify as gay and resented Gay Liberation, both for its politics and its demands on Charley's time. Simultaneously, Charley had intense sexual relationships with several other men, none of whom identified as gay; they were unfailingly demanding, sometimes abusive, and always wanted money.

Decades of juggling such contradictions might well have tempered the politics of a more flexible character. Charley responded in the opposite direction: as the world changed and political gains were made, his repudiation of realpolitik became more staunch; he would admit no compromise. A prophet of a sexually radical New Jerusalem, he grew further and further out of sync with both the politics of the day—as Gay Liberation shifted to the incremental, rights-based approach of gay rights—and a capacity to make sense of, and run, his own life. Alzheimer's was, in retrospect, almost a metaphor for his mind being, for decades, buffeted against the unyielding hull of his ideology, a Platonic ideal of the praiseworthy, unsullied outsider to which no real life could hope to measure up.

It was in his response to HIV/AIDS that one can, in hindsight, see the earliest signs of Charley's fraying, as the utopia he had envisioned—hoped for, fought for—literally died. As the epidemic grew, voices both within and outside of the gay community embraced a type of political and physical holiness doctrine that repudiated the unfettered sexuality Charley believed would save the world. Conservative politicians and clergy turned the epidemic into a sex panic that was aimed not only at gay sex but gay men and gay culture. Charley, on the defensive, doubled down on his position, refused to contemplate nuance. On a panel discussion about HIV in the late 1980s, he sounded his own death knell as a public intellectual: "In the 1960s they asked if you were willing to die for the revolution. Shouldn't we be willing to die for the sexual revolution?" As startling as it is wrongheaded, the provocation was a glimpse into how profoundly HIV/AIDS had unmoored Charley.

He was himself diagnosed with the disease in 1994, though he told almost no one of his HIV status, then or ever. This seemed odd, ironic, and even disingenuous for a man who had no problem discussing the exact details of his sexual life in print and in conversation. The losses of the epidemic continually shook him to the core. His increasingly frequent trips out of the country from the late 1980s onward—to Ecuador, Egypt, Vietnam, and Paris—were a flight from friends dying at home. It came to be a joke that if Charley was going away, someone must be at death's door.

Charley also found it increasingly difficult to embody the role of the provocateur. Many of his commitments—to transformations of sexual relationships and family, to making private sexuality more public—simply were not as shocking as they once had been, for which he had no one to blame but himself: it was, ironically, because of the success of the sexual revolution he had helped imagine, and which his intellectual descendants had translated into more practical terms. Public discussions of sex were now routine in the media. Madonna's 1992 Sex book brought leather and BDSM to mall bookstores and Middle America's coffee tables. By 1998 the explicit details of Bill Clinton and Monica Lewinsky's sexual encounters were permissible daytime television talk. There could hardly be a more concrete measure of cultural change than the fact that discussions of cocksucking moved, in the course of twenty years, from the pages of Fag Rag to CBS.

The same year that Charley was diagnosed with HIV, Gordon died of cancer. Soon after, Charley lost the patience for teaching. For the first time in his career he would complain about being exasperated by his students. After taking several leaves, he retired in 2001. His behavior was also changing. His inclination to pick through sidewalk trash increased and his Cambridge home—already a vast archive of his papers and LGBT ephemera (Yale's Beinecke Library acquired 160 boxes of his papers after he went into the nursing home)—filled with old magazines and broken furniture. Charley's several cats began to breed within the confines of the house, and by 1997 there were thirty of them. An attic room became a litter box. In the heat of the summer, the smell of cat waste would radiate from the house, until eventually the city interceded.

The hoarding had something to do, in Charley's mind, with arresting the passage of time. When questioned about the feline miasma, he said that his childhood home had smelled like a barnyard. At the height of his powers, conversation with Charley was invigorating. Now it centered obsessively on discussions of his sexual exploits, without any connection to a theory or politics of sexuality. The personal had stopped being political—it was now just recitation to shock. Imagine Lear on the heath, transposed to a dilapidating house in Cambridge filled with trash: Charley's rants were no longer prophetic or visionary, but howled into the swirling winds of a new world. It was as though he was trapped in a fractured, funhouse version of the past, where resided all the habitus of a younger Charley but with none of the critical faculties. A trained historian, he could not manage the critical distance to appreciate the changes that time had performed during his own lifetime.

Once the Alzheimer's became more evident, and his living at home became a danger to himself and others, friends took over guardianship and he entered a nursing home. By this time he had forgotten his bitterness and anger, and he had descended pleasantly into his own world of confused, often imagined, memories.

But everything old is new again. I can't help but wish that Charley had been able to hold on for longer, to see youth activists turn from the real politik of gay rights to embrace, yet again, his prophetic vision of a world reborn, with sexual minorities leading the charge. Ironically Charley's dream is more vibrant, and realizable, today than it has been since the beginning of the AIDS epidemic. Gay Liberation, after becoming the gay rights movement, has reemerged as a queer movement that is rejecting gay marriage as the defining issue. Instead, young queer activists are making demands that recall Gay Men's Liberation's manifesto: an end to policing and the carceral state; the right for all people to express their sexual identity and be safe from rape; the end of considerations of skin color, country of origin, and religion in matters of immigration and citizenship. No movement is perfect, but as the first Fag Rag declared, though we are not yet liberated, we are working toward liberation.

No prophet is accepted in his hometown, and even less in his own time. Charley was a visionary who became, tragically, impatient with his vision. Being a prophet comes with burdens and responsibilities, which may be, under some circumstances, unbearable. Yet as activists come to terms with the limitations of a rights-based approach to full liberation, the need for such visionaries is more acute than ever. Oscar Wilde wrote in his 1891 "The Soul of Man Under Socialism": "A map of the world that does not include Utopia is not worth even glancing at, for it leaves out the one country at which Humanity is always landing. And when Humanity lands there, it looks out, and, seeing a better country, sets sail. Progress is the realisation of Utopias."

—Michael Bronski

"The Last Gay Liberationist" was first published December 20th 2017 in the Boston Review

Charles Shively was born in Gobbler's Knob, Ohio in 1937. He enrolled in Harvard in 1955, received his Masters degree from the University of Wisconsin in 1959 and received his PhD from Harvard in 1969. Throughout his teaching career at Boston State College and UMASS Boston, Charley was awarded three Fulbright Research and Teaching Grants sending him to Mexico, Ecuador and Vietnam. In 1971, Charley, Michael Bronski, John Mitzel and Larry Martin formed a radical gay anarchist collective and began publishing the Boston Gay Newspaper: Fag Rag, which ran until the early 1980's publishing 12 of Charleys infamous radical essays. He was a founding member the Good Gay Poets Collective publishing several seminal books of poetry by queer poets outside the mainstream poetry establishment such as Freddie Greenfield's *Were You Always a Criminal?* ruth weiss's *Desert Journals*, Aaron Shurin's broadside *Exorcism of the straight/man/demon* and John Wiener's magnum opus, *Behind the State Capitol*. Shively also published Adrian Stanford's groundbreaking *Black and Queer*, the first book of poetry written by a queer African American poet. Charley also published the *Collected Works of Lysander Spooner* (1971), *A History of the Conception of Death in America, 1650-1860*, his doctoral dissertation (1988), *Calamus Lovers: Walt Whitman's Working Class Camerados* (1987) and *Drum Beats: Walt Whitman's Civil War Boy Lovers* (1989). Charley's only published collection of poems was in *Nuestra Señora de los Dolores: the San Francisco Experience* (1975).

This first edition of *I Have a Poem for You*
was designed and typeset by Erik Lomen
for Bootstrap Press in Summer 2025. The
typeface is Joanna designed by Eric Gill.

www.ingramcontent.com/pod-product-compliance
Lightning Source LLC
Chambersburg PA
CBHW081203170426
43197CB00018B/2908
* 9 7 8 1 9 4 6 7 4 1 1 8 9 *